Nature on the Doorstep

Nature on the Doorstep

A Year of Letters

Angela E. Douglas

Comstock Publishing Associates
an imprint of
Cornell University Press

Ithaca and London

First published 2023 by Cornell University Press

Printed in the United States of America

Library of Congress Cataloging-in-Publication Data

Names: Douglas, A. E. (Angela Elizabeth), 1956– author.
Title: Nature on the doorstep: a year of letters / Angela E. Douglas.
Description: Ithaca: Comstock Publishing Associates, 2023.
Identifiers: LCCN 2022017840 (print) | LCCN 2022017841 (ebook) |
    ISBN 9781501768118 (paperback) | ISBN 9781501768125 (pdf) |
    ISBN 9781501768132 (epub)
Subjects: LCSH: Natural history—New York (State)—Ithaca. | Nature and
    civilization—New York (State)—Ithaca. | LCGFT: Creative nonfiction.
Classification: LCC QH81. D675 2023 (print) | LCC QH81 (ebook) |
    DDC 508.747/71—dc23/eng/20220718
LC record available at https://lccn.loc.gov/2022017840
LC ebook record available at https://lccn.loc.gov/2022017841

Contents

Preface

It all started when we lurched into the March 2020 lockdown. In the uncharted territory of the COVID-19 pandemic, I needed distraction. So I spent a Sunday morning writing a short piece about the preceding week's events in the backyard. Initially, I thought I was indulging is a trivial once-off activity—a rather foolish digression from the important world of human affairs and my never-ending to-do list for work. A thousand words later, I discovered that I was much less anxious, more philosophical about the state of things.

I read out my backyard story to my husband, Jeremy. It made him laugh, and it gave us something other than lockdown anxieties to talk about. Then I wrote an email note to family members saying, "I have started a weekly newsletter about our backyard. Well, I am not sure if it will last, but here is the first installment." I had in mind that this might help us through the few weeks of lockdown before we all returned to normal.

Such naïveté! Throughout the year that followed, the backyard came to dominate our newfound and unchosen stay-at-home lives. This parallel universe, in which the pandemic is never mentioned, offered us entertainment and solace through the endless news cycles of mayhem and moments of horror. Writing about the week's backyard events every Sunday morning became a necessary part of my life. Without any explicit intention, I had constructed a year of weekly natural history essays.

I offer a warm welcome to everyone who happens upon this book. Whether you are in a lull or a storm in your life, I hope you enjoy the read, just as I have enjoyed the writing.

A Note to Readers

I owe you some explanation before we begin. Most importantly, my husband and I are not keen gardeners. In fact, our yard is rather neglected. This is partly because we lead busy lives, but it is also strategic neglect—for reasons that I explore in the postscript.

Our backyard is in the small city of Ithaca in rural upstate New York, where we have lived since moving over a decade ago from the UK to jobs at Cornell University. In February 2008, we made a five-day visit from England to buy a house, an important part of the complex jigsaw for the jobs starting in the summer. It was a crazy plan, but the first house we viewed was perfect. The only unknown was the backyard, which was buried under a foot of snow. We took a gamble and signed on the dotted line, hoping that we had not purchased a scrappy jungle of couch grass and bramble or, worse, the regimented order created by a busy-busy gardener. We were in luck! When we returned to occupy the house in the sweaty heat of summer, we discovered that the previous owners had been minimal maintenance people in the backyard. There was plenty of interesting wildlife, much of which was new to us. We had landed in the right place, a place where we could belong, for the adventure of our new lives in this amazing country.

So, when I came to write my weekly letters about the backyard, my chief recipients were family members living in the UK. As a result, the text is peppered with comparisons to the natural history of the UK, and I occasionally mention quirky aspects of life and customs here in Ithaca and in the US. At least, they are quirky for Brits! Moreover, these letters were written in the spirit of Alistair Cooke's *Letter from America*. I had listened, over decades in the UK, to his radio broadcast every Sunday morning. Each talk was sufficient to itself; it never mattered if I missed an episode, but cumulatively I absorbed a little understanding of the US. My own letters are likewise informal essays rather than communications to specific correspondents. As with Alistair Cooke's letters, you can start reading at any date. On occasion I do refer to previous letters but never ones in the future because, after all, I had no idea what was in store for the coming week or month.

THE LETTERS

March 22, 2020

ON THE HORNS OF A DILEMMA

It was this time last week that we realized we were on the horns of a dilemma. Our troubles related to our bird feeders, which we watch from our dining room table. As we ate our Sunday lunch, a flock of house sparrows consumed the remainder of the food in the birdseed dispenser and the last of the suet in the suet holder. House sparrows lack prudence in their eating habits, very different from our regular customers, the chickadees, the tufted titmice, the downy woodpeckers, and the juncos, and our occasional visitors, the Carolina wrens, the house finches, and the red-bellied woodpeckers. Our dilemma was whether to restock our bird feeders.

As with all problems, extra information—even apparently irrelevant information—can help decision-making. The first issue is our regular customers. Was my list complete? What about the cardinals, who have been singing and displaying for days? Alas, they are not regular customers because our bird feeders are enclosed in wire cages that cardinals are too big to enter, and their stumpy beaks are far too short to reach the food from outside the cage. The wire cages are needed to keep the gray squirrels at bay. The feeders are suspended, side by side, from nails on a low branch of our red maple tree, just next to the deck and, as I've already mentioned, with an excellent view from the dining room. The squirrels play on the tree. They groom themselves on the branch holding the feeders, and then lean down, a greedy glint in the eye. One squirrel sways precariously in a tight hug around the feeder, presumably hoping to knock it to the ground. Another squirrel bares its teeth and chews at the metal lid. So far, every display of gymnastics and brute force has been to no avail, not just this year but every year.

Why do we have the house sparrow dilemma? Why haven't we been visited by house sparrows throughout the winter? The reason is simple. Our local flock of house sparrows lives in a big forsythia hedge at the bottom of the road, and these birds don't venture far in cold weather. We don't know why the sparrows are fair-weather visitors. Perhaps they are fed by the owners of the forsythia hedge until it gets warm; perhaps they don't like to fly far in the cold. Whatever the reason, the sparrows came with a welcome improvement to the weather, several days of glorious sunshine and blue skies. As we tour the estate, we see spring coming early.

Now this requires some explanation. What is our estate? The backyard is roughly seventy-five feet long and forty-five feet wide, comprising a rectangle of lawn facing roughly south, with a tarmac driveway down the east edge to a garage in the southeast corner. We are bounded by close neighbors to the east, south, and west, separated by a fence (aka squirrel runway) and, along part of the west side, a privet hedge. We have flower borders all around the edge. Our mature trees are the red maple close to the house by the deck, an overhanging box elder in our east neighbor's yard, a black walnut at the southern end, and a group of Norway spruce and Scotch pine in the southeast corner. We have planted some extra trees, including birch, eastern hop hornbeam, serviceberry, eastern hemlock, and eastern redbud, over the last decade and all are saplings. Encouragingly, all the young trees appear to have survived the winter with this season's buds starting to swell.

Snowdrops, crocuses, and winter aconites are in flower, and the violets on the raised bed on the east of the backyard are already a glorious deep purple.

So, let's go back to the beginning. As we watched the house sparrows demolish the food and leave, we decided not to refill. Then a female red-bellied woodpecker arrived, poked and pecked into the empty space of the suet holder, obviously perturbed. She left. Her partner followed, and he was also visibly put out by the state of affairs. The next in line were the downy woodpeckers, scurrying low along the branch, down to the empty suet holder. Last was a Carolina wren who jumped excitedly around in the suet holder, flew off, and then returned to repeat its antics. We got the message. Directly after lunch, Jeremy refilled the bird feeders.

We made the right decision. Although the house sparrows were back within ten minutes of the refill, they did not consume all the food in a day. On Thursday we had a magical visitation by a male pileated woodpecker. The pileated looks like something out of *Jurassic Park*. He is about the same size as a crow and, like a crow, black but with white under the wings, a bright red crest, and a beak as big as its head. He hung upside down at the bottom of the suet holder and jabbed repeatedly at the suet with great ferocity, showering suet pieces in all directions. His mate, a little smaller and with a red bonnet, was in attendance, rocking her way down the trunk of the tree. All our regular customers had cleared off, and even the house sparrows retreated to the tips of the maple branches and the privet hedge, where they chattered excitedly.

So, a week after the refill, the suet holder is empty and the seed holder nearly so, courtesy of the house sparrows and a pileated woodpecker. It is time to move on. Spring is upon us, even though it is forecast to snow tonight. Our dilemma is resolved, and our regular customers must forage elsewhere.

March 29, 2020

SPRING IS COMING . . .

They were brave words, last week, about the start of spring. The threatened overnight snow happened, and we woke on Monday morning to a thin white covering, not enough to make a snowman but certainly enough to remind us that the pendulum between winter and summer is swinging wide. But this pendulum has a bias, and summer will win in the end.

I have kept up what Jeremy grandly calls my daily half-hour run just before lunch. Of course, it is more of an ambling trot. To avoid the day-long parade of dog walkers on the street, I trot up and down our drive, which runs north to south by the east fence. This gives me plenty of practice of trotting turns because our drive is rather short. More importantly, I have a brief thirty minutes to absorb each day's mood. On Monday the mood was gloves and dribbling snow. I got caught by a hailstorm on Tuesday, trotted under gray skies on Wednesday and Friday and in persistent rain on Saturday. Thursday was this week's single day of spring—clear blue skies, brilliant sunshine, and warm enough to discard my coat at twenty minutes. Thursday felt very special.

So, what have I absorbed during my daily trots? First, I thought about US culture. You would imagine that our tarmacked drive-way to the garage would be for the car. But that makes no sense because the driveway is too narrow for any car. No, the garage is for storing all your myriad of complex, noisy machinery that you need for the backyard, from the outdoor grill, through the snowblower and leaf blower, to winter sports gear and then your summer water sports equipment. And what do we store in the garage? During the winter, our supersized wooden deck table and bench, inherited from the previous owners, fill most of the space. And then we have a lawnmower, spade, and rake, a trowel, and a rusty pair of secateurs. We also keep the dustbins (they are called garbage cans here) in the garage to protect them from the raccoons. Jeremy is sympathetic about raccoons (except when they go for the garbage), but I see a raccoon and, correctly, think one word: rabies!

But one rarely sees raccoons by day, thank goodness, and my daily trots last week were certainly raccoon-free.

Despite the mostly atrocious weather, the raised bed by the east fence has, each day, had more violets in flower than on the previous day. We now have a wonderful display of more than one hundred deep-purple flowers, plus one white violet. The forsythia bush next to the garage was just a tangled mass of thin brown twigs on Monday, but from Thursday onward it has been tinged in yellow. It will be in bloom very soon, I am sure. Our first scillas are in flower, brilliant blue, one just next to one of the composters and two haphazardly located in the lawn. It is the start of the season to watch your step on our lawn. Advance warning: step watching will become more interesting as the weeks progress.

The birds that kept me company through my trot varied from one day to the next. Monday and Tuesday, the real-winter days of the week, were the days of the blue jays. A group of six to eight blue jays flew around from one tall tree to another, enthusiastically squawking and screaming to one another the entire time. Blue jays do this all year round, for they always have something to say. Well, almost always. There was an exception this morning. A perfectly silent blue jay on a branch of the red maple. He was bobbing up and down on his skinny black legs, presumably trying to impress his lady love.

The robins have been back for several weeks now. Our robins are, of course, not the same as the European robins that adorn Christmas cards, but a kind of thrush with an orange breast extending to its belly. Robins abandon us for several months of the winter. They may not travel far. Some go into the woods, and many go south, perhaps only to the south of New York State. Their return to the backyard is an early sign of spring. They have been very busy on our lawn, often as singletons or in small groups, foraging for worms and upending dead leaves for insects and spiders for some days now. But by Wednesday and especially Thursday, they had sorted themselves out and we now have our one resident pair. Well, there will be some male incursions, but any wayward male will be chased off in great alarm. On Thursday, our day of spring, I shared my driveway run with our robin pair. The two birds were so busy attending to each other that they neglected my regular back-and-forth. The male took center stage on the drive, strutting around and shaking his wings amorously at the female. She appeared to be impressed. At least, she ignored me as much as he did, as I trotted along the edge, to keep out of their way. They also have their territory in place. Since midweek we have been hearing the daily early morning robin song. He starts about an hour before dawn, always the first, and his song is the most boring thrush song you can imagine.

I will finish with some birds that passed through on Monday. They were mainly to the front. The road was invaded by a large flock of grackles, presumably on their journey northward. They were in the tall maple of one neighbor on the other side of the street, and then foraging on the slope of rough grass by the next neighbor's house, all the while maintaining contact with that hopelessly unmusical grackle call. They stayed for a few hours to recharge, and then they were gone.

April 5, 2020

WORDSWORTH'S FLOWERS

Ithacans love to tell you that every year is different. Then a pregnant pause, and then an outpouring of "the year when there was frost in August," "the year when we celebrated Mother's Day (always the second Sunday in May) with ten inches of snow," and so on. Yet again, this year is different.

The special thing about this year is that the daffodils came into bloom this week. Compared to many years, this is seriously early. All too often, daffodils are a frustration. They burst into flower when the weather switches from winter to summer in late April, and then they wilt within days from heat exhaustion. And they appear at exactly the same time as everything else, the tulips, serviceberry tree and redbud, apple and cherry blossom. But not this year. The daffodils have come into flower in the right order, after the snowdrops are done, as the winter aconites and crocuses are starting to wane, and together with the forsythia.

We have been checking our daffodils daily, from the first shoots in the snow, through the slowly emerging buds, and finally, early this week, most came into flower. There is a dense clump of ten flowers just below our violet patch by the east wall, and a dozen flowers below the crab apple tree in the front. We also have some daffodils in the grass near the front door, but these daffodils have troubles. The front of the house faces roughly north and, until about the March equinox, the sun is so low and sets so early that this area gets no sun at all. So the snow lingers, and if there is any melt, it then refreezes as hard, heavy ice. Compounding this disadvantage, we shovel the winter snow from the drive onto the front lawn (it has to go somewhere . . .), leaving these daffodils in deep snow when other parts of our yard have little or no snow at all. For some years now, these troubled daffodils have been entirely vegetative—leaves but no flowers. I have been adding compost every year, and this year—alleluia!—we have twenty buds, two of which came into flower this morning.

I cannot help but think of William Wordsworth's host of golden daffodils, even though our daffodils aren't the wild daffodils that flashed upon his inward eye. Instead, we have a wonderful mongrel mix of garden varieties, inherited from the previous owners of our house, some with white petals, others with deep-yellow petals. All our daffodils have a yellow corolla. Thank goodness, none of them have the ugly double or triple corollas.

The other big event of the week is also Wordsworthian. Apparently his favorite flower was the lesser celandine. We have celandines in profusion, a few flowers this last week and anticipating many more in the next few days. The lesser celandine is no more native to the US than the daffodil, and it is definitely an uninvited guest. Several years ago, we spotted a few plants between the deck and maple tree. It has since spread, forming a dense mat of glossy leaves. Until this year we were saying, "Oh good, what a lovely show under our maple tree!" And it still is. But in the last year, the celandines have got to the bank along the east fence, running south from our violet patch to our forsythia bush. This bank has long been the preserve of marjoram, with summer flowers much loved by bees and other insects. Until this year, the main threat to the marjoram has been ground ivy, which I have carefully plucked out by hand. But now we have the phalanx of lesser celandine which smothers everything in its path.

Several years ago, I planted two *Sedum spectabile* alongside the marjoram. They flower in September and are perfect for the late summer bees. One has been doing well, but the other has needed more tending. Yesterday afternoon, I spotted the tip of a leaf of "the other." This year's growth had been completely submerged in celandine. So I set to it with a trowel, to create a *cordon sanitaire* around the struggling sedum. I discovered that the celandines have tiny tubers, myriads of them all close to the surface. No wonder they move in and take over. I did my very best to extricate the little white pearls of celandine tubers without damaging the already suffering sedum, but the coming days will tell how successful I have been. That done, I realized that our marjoram is also in danger, and so I dug out some of the celandine. Jeremy and I will need to have a chat about whether to try to remove all of the celandine from the east bank.

So much for Wordsworth's favorite plant. But then, it didn't end well for him either. It was decided that he loved the lesser celandine so much that it should be engraved on his tombstone. But the administrators (bless them, they never change!) arranged for a carving of the greater celandine, which, of course, is a poppy and only distantly related to the lesser celandine, which is in the buttercup family.

April 12, 2020

VULTURES AND RABBITS

It has been a week in two parts. The early week was warm and sunny, reaching the dizzy heights of 60°F (16°C). We even had lunch perched on the deck, accompanied by early bees feasting on celandine nectar under the maple tree. But the weather forecast had warned us not to bring out the deck table from the garage. By midweek we were back to the thirties (minus 1 to 4°C). The transition was a classic Ithaca weather swing. The wind got up. All the trees were shaking, and the pines in the southeast corner sounded as if they were sighing, as they always do when it is windy. The sky was pale blue, then within ten minutes steel gray all over, then back to clear sky and so on. We like to think of our local patch as a complicated landscape with its gorges and waterfalls, steep hills and deep lakes, but our weather system operates on a far grander scale. There is no meaningful barrier between us and the high Arctic or the Great Plains because the mountains run north to south. (We are north of the Appalachians and west of their northerly extensions, the Catskills and Adirondacks.) This week's weather switch was typically fast, and we hunkered down under the strong northerly winds that brought rain, sleet, and snow.

At the height of the weather change, we watched a group of turkey vultures circling overhead. Turkey vultures are summer visitors, but they are resident downstate. So they don't have far to come and they can make snap decisions. They were even with us last Christmas, making use of a brief period of unseasonably warm weather. But what were they doing aloft during our weather switch? No other bird was out, all were taking refuge from the wind. This was not a good time to be foraging, and they were behaving much as they do when gathering to migrate south in the fall. Perhaps they were getting themselves in good order for a tactical retreat southward in advance of the wintry weather. Consistent with that, we haven't seen them in the last few days at all. But they will be back, and we will enjoy them through the summer soaring above us on their enormous wings, wingtips spread out like fingers.

We have had another visitor in the last week. It was on Tuesday, and it was a rabbit. During the winter, we don't tend to have any rabbits in our yard. We think they stay in the patch of undeveloped land beyond our southern neighbor, probably sheltering through the bad weather in an abandoned woodchuck burrow or a dogwood thicket. We were glad to see him (yes, almost certainly a male). Of course, just one rabbit because he is not a European rabbit but an eastern cottontail, a solitary and a much more timid beast than the European. The cottontails are smaller and leaner with longer legs (more like a hare), and they can zigzag at great speed when needed. But our visitor appeared very much at ease, selecting clover and dandelion leaves from our lawn. All our young trees are protected by rather ugly mesh, and after the rabbit had left, I checked that the mesh was firmly in place down to soil level. Much as we love rabbit visitations, one brief circular meal of nutritious plant tissue just under the bark could kill one of our precious birch saplings, a hop hornbeam, or a serviceberry tree.

On our tour of the estate next day, we spotted that the flourishing leaves of the grape hyacinth in the bed under the kitchen window had been neatly trimmed to 80 percent of their original length. So I sprayed the grape hyacinth with our all-organic spray of decayed "egg solids" and garlic, which makes the plants distasteful to rabbits and deer. Most plants in most Ithacan backyards are naturally deer-resistant, and anything else is an indulgence. My sedums, mentioned last week, are one of my few indulgences. But I digress from the rabbit. We are now keeping a daily watch on our grape hyacinth leaves, our bad egg spray at the ready.

The grape hyacinths are not our only rabbit worry. We also worry for the rabbit. We have another regular visitor that we wish would just stay at home. It is a "new" cat. It is black and, although well cared for, it has a decidedly lean and hungry look. We aren't sure if it is genuinely new. It may have expanded its range, following a change in the next-door (east) household, from two noisy dogs to a pet-free zone. Whatever the cause, the recent visitations from the cat harass our squirrels, deter our rabbit, and presumably take their toll on our juncos and chipmunks. The cat is not welcome.

But our rabbit visitor will have nothing to fear from the turkey vultures when they return. Turkey vultures feed strictly on carrion, and they are renowned for their remarkable sense of smell, detecting their next meal of dead meat from a great height.

April 19, 2020

BLOOM WHERE YOU ARE PLANTED

Our big event of the week was to wake up on Thursday morning to a snowy wonderland. These days, I do the weekly grocery shop first thing on Thursday mornings. I sighed a heavy February sigh, swept the snow off the car, and then spent ten minutes scraping the good quarter-inch layer of ice from the car windows before I could set off.

Snow at this time of year is not especially surprising, and it came in a week when spring was on hold. We were below freezing every night and never got above 40°F (4°C) during the day. So our violets, celandines, and daffodils have not progressed at all, and a few daffodils are still in bud in the front. The violets and celandines tolerated the weather very well, but the snow was wet and heavy, weighing down our daffodils, some of which have not recovered.

But what I really want to write about today is a bush that came into flower just before our backyard went "into the fridge" for the week. It is the spicebush, *Lindera benzoin*. It sounds as if it should be an exotic, perhaps coming from the Indian subcontinent, but it is a native. In early spring before its leaves develop, the spicebush is covered in little clusters of lemon-yellow flowers. We may not have pussy willow or hazel catkins but, gosh, we do have spicebush. We see it, now and again (not super-common), in the woods, and also in backyards all over Ithaca.

Our spicebush is a great survivor. The story starts a few years after we moved to this house. We decided to "do something about" the bed at the south end of the backyard. Our priority was to replace the aged and unproductive plants with redbud and hemlock, both natives to this area. The plants to be ousted included an unidentifiable specimen that appeared to be following the instruction of George's Grandma (of Roald Dahl's *George's Marvelous Medicine* fame): to grow downward. Each year, it got smaller and had fewer leaves. It certainly was not blooming where it was planted. So we dug it up in a small clump of soil (its roots did not appear to have grown downward) and put it by the west fence, intending to throw it out. There must have been a dose of George's medicine in all of this. The diminutive plant started to grow. Within a couple of days, without its even being properly planted, new leaf buds developed and the shoot tips extended. Well, it was mid-May, the time of year when everything grows like crazy, but this was super-crazy. So we planted it, there and then. It put on lots of vegetative growth in that first year but, what with one thing and another, we didn't get round to identifying it. Next spring it bloomed and, inescapably, it was a spicebush. We had planted it where it would bloom.

I wish that I could say that our spicebush has lived happily ever after. It is certainly thriving, getting bigger every year. But it did have an accident, in the fall of its second year after the transplantation. One day, one of the two main stems of the spicebush sheared off. Okay, spicebushes have very weak wood, but this was awful. This unbalanced half-bush would be vulnerable in the winter wind, and the long gaping wound was an invitation for every late season fungus. We did not think it would survive the winter—and we were wrong. You can see the scar of the accident today, but otherwise, you would never guess, some six or seven years later, that this plant started off in the wrong place and then was reduced to a half-bush.

What was the cause of the accident? It was suggested to us by the tree man, who, one year, cut back the maple tree by the deck, that a deer jumped over the fence and landed in the bush. He is a true Ithacan. If in doubt, blame the deer. Well, that is marginally more plausible than suggesting that George's Grandma jumped over the fence, but it must have been a deer that made no mark in the soil. I suspect that our invigorated spicebush outgrew its strength in the first year in the right place, and the soft wood split apart under its own weight.

Perhaps I will have a chance another time to expand on why I think our spicebush needed to be planted in the right place to bloom. But I can finish here by explaining why *Lindera benzoin* is called a spicebush. It is a laurel, and its leaves have a lovely near-lemon smell. The spicebush is closely related to the famous sassafras tree, which reaches its northern limit near us. The root of the sassafras is used to flavor homemade root beers and the gumbo dishes in New Orleans. But discretion is well advised because the active ingredient, safrole, is carcinogenic. For the last sixty years, commercial root beers have been flavored with black birch bark or, more frequently, a bunch of artificial flavors.

I will close with a note about the title of today's letter. "Bloom where you are planted" is written on a little wooden sign hanging on the front porch of a house in a different neighborhood of town called Fall Creek. (You may need translation here. Many old houses have what's called a porch, which is a veranda extending the full length of the front of the house, a place where you can sit and watch the world go by.) In many ways, Fall Creek defines the self-image of Ithacans. Fall Creek is resplendent with window posters and front yard signs proclaiming that Black Lives Matter, Hate Has No Home Here, Every Person Is Legal, and more. It is a jolly and friendly neighborhood. On the front porch of Bloom Where You Are Planted, there is a sagging sofa that has endured the seasons for many years and likely sustains various rodent and insect families, together with a motley collection of untended, slowly dying potted plants. Every time I walk past this house, I remind myself how important it is to be planted in the right place.

April 26, 2020

What on earth was I talking about in March about an early spring this year? We have just had our second week of wintry weather. A biting northerly wind has given us a wind chill well below freezing, and on three days I finished my pre-lunch driveway run shaking the snow off my hat and coat before stepping back into the house.

So each day, I trotted up the drive in the face of an arctic wind that then buffeted me back down the drive. And each day, I passed the same waning violets on the east wall, the daffodils bludgeoned by the elements, and the brave grape hyacinths under the kitchen window. It was truly a week of winter dregs.

To take my mind off the atrocious weather, I listened. Every day, I was accompanied by one distinctive voice, which I heard in the box elder tree, on the fence, on the garage roof, or just echoing around in the wind. It was the gray squirrels, one of four squirrel species in our neck of the woods. The others are the American red, also a regular visitor to our backyard, and the flying squirrel and fox squirrel, both of which prefer woodland habitats. There is also the Douglas's squirrel, which is restricted to the West Coast—that's a different story.

When we first came to the US, so much was different, but I told myself that at least the gray squirrels would be the same. How wrong I was! We can all agree that Thomas Brocklehurst, the banker from near Macclesfield in Cheshire, was very foolish to return from his 1876 business trip to New York City with a pair of gray squirrels. But he and all the stupid rich people who copied him were doubly foolish to choose peculiarly stupid gray squirrels. Gray squirrels here are much, much more fun than in the UK.

For a start, they yabber nonstop. I trotted with gritted teeth and hunched shoulders to the tune of squirrel tooth chattering, punctuated by high-pitched screams and the fiercest rapidly repeated kuk-kuk-kuks. Of course, their teeth weren't chattering from the cold, and they weren't screaming at the elements. Squirrels are made of far firmer stuff than me. The endless jabber is mostly saying Keep Out to other squirrels—I haven't yet succumbed to cat or car.

When our squirrels aren't holding forth from a high vantage point or chasing around in the trees, they are on the ground burying or unearthing tidbits. They are meant to do this mostly in fall and spring, but in reality it is a daily, year-round business. Squirrels have nuts on the brain. It is tempting to think that their tiny brains are holding a vast amount of information about the age and location of every buried morsel. Has someone found that black walnut which I buried next to the dogwood tree last month? Is my cache of maple seeds getting past its sell-by date? But squirrel scientists have found that gray squirrels find nuts that the researchers buried as swiftly as their own nuts, suggesting that, although they have nuts on their brains, it ain't any particular nuts.

One consequence of the nut obsession is that squirrels are a regular gardening companion. As I do the weeding, I see one or several squirrels watching me from a safe distance. Why does this human dig into soil and turn over the earth? The only possible explanation is that she is burying nuts. As I put the trowel back into the garage and return to the house, the squirrels descend to ground level. They check over even the smallest sign of disturbed soil, grubbing it up and leaving a scattering of shallow pits. Of course, usually they come away empty-handed.

But every now and again, that trowel is used to bury goodies. We have a small Colorado spruce tree (not a native, a western species that is widely planted because it is very hardy) between the front door and the drive. It is a welcome splash of blue-green color in midwinter but rather dull for the rest of the year. In several years, I have planted crocus bulbs or similar just in front of the spruce, but nothing has come up. Initially I attributed my failure to rotting by soil fungi in the wet fall or spring, but then I thought about our teeth-chattering friends. Last autumn, Jeremy bought me a pack of scilla bulbs. It was an opportunity to try again by the Colorado spruce tree. I decided to plant the bulbs deep, flatten the soil firmly, and then sprinkle the area liberally with an all-organic stinky mix of mint oil, rosemary oil, and cedar oil. I kept a watchful eye through the winter. Every time frost heave moved the soil, I stamped it flat and added more of the stinky mix. This spring, we have a glorious show of deep-blue scillas. Perhaps, just perhaps, I beat the gray squirrels.

Ithaca hasn't always been a welcoming place for gray squirrels. Anna Comstock's wonderful and justly famous *Handbook of Nature Study*, written here in Ithaca (Comstock 1911), has five pages on the American red squirrel, including suggestions for student lessons. She does mention black squirrels, which she explains were common when she was a child but had since been exterminated by shotgun-wielding hunters. I am pretty sure that her black squirrels were a melanic population of the gray squirrel. If the gray was at all evident, it would be the first choice for a nature study lesson. We should be glad that the gray squirrel is back and that our local gray squirrels are safe from the shotgun, described by Anna Comstock as "the most cowardly and unfair invention of the human mind."

Altogether, the squirrels kept me amused during my driveway trots in the winter dregs of the last week. I am sure that they, like me, can't wait for summer!

May 3, 2020

THE ENGLISH DAISY

When I first arrived in Ithaca in the heat of early August 2008, I noticed that the back lawn had no daisies. Sensible plants, I thought, keeping low through the summer heat. They'll be back once it cools down. But come September, daisies—the delight of any right-minded gardener—weren't to be seen in our backyard or anywhere else locally. I had been warned that everyone who makes a big life change has a defining "Oh my God, what have I done?" moment. For me, it was the moment when the penny dropped, and I realized that *Bellis perennis* has not come to Ithaca. No primroses, no bluebells, no harebells, and, the greatest loss of all, no daisies. At the time, I suspected that the local climate was just too harsh for daisies. But a few years ago, we discovered that it is not just Ithaca missing out. *Bellis perennis* is sometimes planted here as an ornamental (the so-called English daisy) and has occasionally escaped, but it is not widespread in North America. For example, it isn't even mentioned in *Wild Urban Plants of the Northeast* by Peter Del Tredici (2010). Don't be taken in by the title. This book should be on everyone's list of top-ten books written by a US author. It is accurate, beautifully written, full of fun information, and illustrated with photographs that capture the habits of each plant perfectly, albeit often in unpromising situations. For example, did you know that ground ivy (the bane of our marjoram patch) was brought over to America on purpose and cultivated as an alternative to hops for beer making? But I digress from the gaping English daisy–shaped hole in the local garden flora.

It was in the first late April/early May after I arrived in the US that a sea of purple at the far end of the lawn suddenly emerged. It was a native, the meadow violet, *Viola papilionacea* (what a lovely name). And the meadow violet blooms on the back lawn at this time every year. Not just our backyard, but it is everywhere—except, of course, under regimes where the winter is spent oiling lawn mower blades and planning campaigns of chemical warfare to ensure a perfectly smooth, textureless lawn of green velvet. Over the years, we have nurtured our meadow violets, and delayed the first mow until after they have set seed. Now the entire back lawn is a glory of violet, and they are doing well in the front too. For the sake of accuracy, the violets that have been blooming on the east wall in recent weeks (see March 22), and are now fully over, are the same species. We aren't sure why the meadow violets on the wall always flower early. Perhaps it is something to do with the thin layer of soil on the wall, which dries out very quickly.

Because we delay the first mow till late May and then mow only sparingly, our lawn is the most wonderful floral display. Almost all our lawn flowers are in the Del Tredici book and, apart from the meadow violet, they will be familiar to any Brit, meaning that they were likely brought, accidentally or by design, by early English colonists. Coming into flower at the same time as the violet is our old friend the dandelion. Alongside the meadow violets and dandelions, hairy bittercress, red dead nettle, field forget-me-nots, and both birdeye and thyme-leaf speedwells are all flourishing. Note for those who care: the birdeye speedwell is *Veronica persica*. Jeremy calls it the field speedwell and Americans call it the Persian speedwell, referring to the germander speedwell as the birdeye. What a muddle!

I am sure you can appreciate that, just at present, our daily tour of the estate is the greatest pleasure—and today temperatures are set to reach 70°F (21°C). We are not the only ones to enjoy it. Most evenings, the buck cottontail visits to chomp his evening meal and groom himself in readiness for the night. One time, he was accompanied by a female. Their courtship mostly involved feeding well apart, studiously ignoring each other. Then he dashed at her head-on. Just before he reached her, she jumped over him. This was repeated another two times, before they retreated out of sight under the maple tree.

On the last day of April, it rained. We were told it was some three inches of rain (phew, not snow this time!), and we can well believe it. Rivers of water raced down the road (we live on an east-to-west slope that non-Ithacans would call a steep hill), puddles expanded on the drive and lawn, and our basement sump pump whirred repeatedly. The robins were very busy through the long downpour, enjoying a feast of worms and insects that were escaping from death by drowning in the soil. Our rabbit stolidly ate his solitary evening meal, despite getting desperately wet. Everything else was taking shelter.

Early morning of May Day was bright and fresh, the day after the flood. Our pair of robins were enjoying a breakfast of rich pickings, but at the back of the lawn there was another thrush, much smaller and behaving just like a song thrush in Britain. It was a hermit thrush, with large dark splotches on its pale breast and a reddish stripe on the outer edge of the tail. A first for our estate! Hermit thrushes are summer visitors that we occasionally see in woodland. This individual was using our backyard as a pit stop on its long journey, perhaps from the Carolinas or even as far south as Guatemala, to its summer residence somewhere between here and halfway up Canada. What a wonderful way to start a new month.

May 10, 2020

BUD BURST!

Today is the second Sunday of May, and so Mother's Day in the US. People take this national holiday very seriously, and the 2020 Mother's Day weekend is turning into something that no one will forget. I am confident that in ten years' time Ithacans will say, "And then there was the spring of 2020. That was the spring when the bomb cyclone hit on Mother's Day weekend." With a sudden and massive drop in pressure at our latitudes, air from the northwest of Canada has rushed down and swept across the continent, where there is no natural barrier to stop it. Since Friday afternoon, we have had snow and hail, sometimes in driving winds of up to forty miles per hour, and the temperatures have dropped below freezing. It is calmer today, and a bit warmer, but it is set to deteriorate again on Monday and Tuesday. There's a lot of excitement that we may beat the low temperature record of 22°F (minus 5.5°C) for today's date in 1947, although I don't think we will. To give you a sense of things, the local high temperature record for this weekend is 93°F (34°C) in 1889.

But you must be getting sick of hearing about our atrocious weather, just as we are sick of experiencing it. So, I will turn to the really important events: what is happening in our backyard. Most people would say that pride of place must go to bud burst of the maples. There are maple trees in every direction, and all are coming into leaf, a wonderful pale green wash over branches that have been bare for so many months. I will write more about that in a moment, but I must first mention my personal top hits of the week.

For me, first place goes to the serviceberry tree, which is coming into flower. Our tree is the smooth serviceberry *Amelanchier laevis*, a native to our parts. You can find this species in the Collins *Field Guide to the Trees of Britain and Northern Europe* (Mitchell 1974), where it is called snowy mespil with the explanation that it has escaped from gardens to Surrey heathlands. The flowers are wonderful, with strap-shaped petals in brilliant white. The flowers appear so vivid because the emerging leaves are dull brown, presumably to avoid visual cues for marauding insect herbivores. And the flowers last for just two to three days. So lovely, and then they are gone.

I will get to the maple tree, I promise, but second place must go to another small tree, the eastern redbud, *Cercis canadensis*. No sign of leaves yet, but the branches of our redbud at the southern end of the backyard are tinged with purple. Myriads of bright purple buds arising directly from the branches will soon open into equally bright-pink pea-like flowers. And in every direction from the house, there are similar small trees swathed in purple. The redbud is loved by Ithacans, who plant it freely, and the redbud loves Ithaca, where it seeds equally freely. The redbud is a native, abundant at the edges and in clearings of our forests. Why is it so special for us? Well, the flowers persist for two weeks or more, so it is not a story of transience. It is more of an ancient history story. Its sister species in Europe is the Judas tree. One of the glories of our personal ancient history (living in the UK) was April holidays in Greece. The Judas trees were always in bloom, mostly around famous archaeological sites. The main thing I remember about our visit to Olympia was the Judas trees, ditto for Delphi and the Asclepeion at Epidaurus. It is very special to have our very own near–Judas tree show here in the US city of Ithaca, namesake of Greece's Ithaca.

And last, there is our red maple tree by the deck. This large tree is coming into leaf, all its branches decked in the most glorious light green. Maples are everywhere in Ithaca, some planted and many self-seeded, and they dominate our deciduous forests too. But it hasn't always been so. Until about a century ago, the dominant deciduous tree in much of the local forests was the American chestnut. Then, in 1904, a fungal pathogen, the chestnut blight, *Cryphonectria parasitica*, arrived with a cargo of the Chinese chestnut trees, and swept across the country, killing the shoots of every American chestnut tree (the fungus causes mild or no symptoms in the Chinese chestnut). The devastation was terrible for years, as is illustrated by a grainy photograph in Anna Comstock's *Handbook of Nature Study* (1911), and then various species of maple spread to occupy the space vacated by the chestnut. We occasionally see small chestnut sprouts in the forests. That is because the fungus doesn't kill the roots and it can take a while for the fungus to find the shoots. It seems that the fungal spores are everywhere, and so the disease will invariably take hold in saplings within a decade of emerging above ground. We are all the poorer for the loss of the American chestnut, but thank goodness the maples stepped into the breach.

Sugar maples and red maples have been harvested by the peoples of North America since for always. Not for their fruits: the maple keys are nothing compared to the nuts of the chestnut, which were eaten just like the nuts of the European sweet chestnut. No, maples are harvested for their syrup. A friend who runs a

mixed farm is always preoccupied by the weather during the sug-
aring season, anytime from mid-February to mid-April. She needs
a sharp overnight frost followed by brilliant sunshine for good sap
flow. Collection is very much in the hands of the weather gods, but
boiling it all down to a pure, uncontaminated syrup requires real
skill. Trade, whether at the local farmers' market or via your carefully cultivated website, depends on a product that is sediment-
free, flows with just the right gloopiness, has a heavenly aroma,
and tastes like paradise on your customers' waffles and bacon.

Back to our maple tree, which serves two important functions
(not sap-tapping) for us. Our bird feeders are on a low horizontal
branch, conveniently positioned for excellent views from the dining room, and in the summer heat it provides a leafy shade for our
meals on the deck. Roll on, summer!

There is a big omission from this account. The omission towers
over the yard, gaunt, leafless branches against the sky. The black
walnut tree is for another week.

May 17, 2020

AND NOW IT'S SUMMER

The switch was thrown on Wednesday and we have summer. We walk into the backyard to a chorus of birdsong that seems to stretch out for miles and miles and miles.

A clue that something was happening came on Tuesday. During my run (which, unlike Monday's, was not in hail but still bitterly cold), I noticed that the juncos were behaving strangely. Our resident juncos are perhaps a little bigger than a British robin and the ultimate ground birds, dark gray to black on top with a white belly and a fetching white tail stripe. All year round they hop around on the driveway, and sit under the forsythia and privet hedge, keeping watch for cats. On this Tuesday morning, five or six of them were messing around high up in the maple tree, repeatedly making high-pitched metallic chip noises. Over lunch, Jeremy guessed, I am sure correctly, that they were migrating juncos. Juncos occupy most of the continent, but they are mainly migratory, overwintering in the US and breeding in Canada. We live in that narrow latitudinal sliver where the juncos stay put for the year (so narrow that, for example, they are winter visitors in New York City). It appears that the movers and stayers don't mix, and the many migrants fly over us—although a few stopped briefly in our maple tree last Tuesday. And that would explain why these juncos were behaving weirdly.

These juncos were interlopers, and soon gone. I wonder exactly where they came from, and where they were going.

And then it was Wednesday, much warmer. We now had deep-pink blossom on the venerable crab apple tree in the front of our house, and a female Baltimore oriole visited, working the flowers for nectar. She has been back repeatedly over the last few days. Well, we think she was female, but it takes two years for the black head and bright orange belly of the males to develop. So that grayish head and pale orange may have been a female or a first-year male. (First-year males can father clutches, and that can confuse bird-watchers, although clearly not female orioles.) Over the last few days, we have also seen definitive males flying at speed, always at speed, through the backyard. They have come all the way from Florida, where they overwinter, and it would be lovely if they stayed with us for the summer this year.

By Thursday, a regular summer visitor was back in town. The catbird, also from Florida or thereabouts, is a little smaller than the British blackbird and a kind of mockingbird. So it has a long tail that it flicks up and down, and lots of songs in its repertoire. It can mew like a cat, bubble like water, and rattle like a stone in a tin can, and it imitates other birds far better than a starling. If in doubt, that birdsong is a catbird. But it is often difficult to confirm because catbirds play it cool. They tend to hide away in vegetation and they are superb ventriloquists—is it over here, or over there, or perhaps behind us? It is a sure sign of summer that our catbirds are back.

Friday was the day that the house wren arrived. We've not seen a house wren in the yard before, so this is very special—and it is still with us, at least through to our sunny breakfast on the deck this morning. Let's just take stock of this one because wrens are like woodpeckers—there are lots of species in America. The British wren is called the winter wren here. We have seen and heard it in the local forests, but I don't recall ever seeing it in our backyard. The winter wren is just one of nine species in the US, including five in New York State. (The cactus wren of the southwestern deserts wouldn't exactly work in Ithaca.) In the backyard, we most commonly see the Carolina wren, which is resident. The house wren, however, is a summer visitor. It is a little larger than the winter wren, and it has a longish tail and an outrageously loud and complex song of rattles and trills. Yes, a perfect wren, and pure pleasure to host on our estate.

By this time, our weather system was struggling with the increase in temperature. It was time for a thunderstorm, our first summer thunderstorm of the year, together with torrential rain through Friday evening. Water, sun, warmth—and every plant had grown another half-inch by Saturday morning. Our crab apple blossom coped well with the storm, but the brilliant white blossom (possibly pear) in the backyard of our westward neighbor took a thrashing. It had been in flower for only a few days, and we saw at our Saturday lunch on the deck that the blossom was ragged and browning, with a steady trickle of petals falling to the ground. No good for orioles—but apparently a feast for insect-loving warblers. Perhaps the sudden deterioration in the blossom got the small flower-inhabiting insects and spiders on the move.

One very special species visiting our neighbor's tree is the Nashville warbler. These birds have come all the way from southern Mexico and are likely passing through to Canada. It is designated uncommon in the bird book. We were also delighted to see several yellow warblers, truly as bright yellow as a canary with red streaking down its front. Unlike the Nashvilles, the yellow warbler is common. It has a delightfully clear song, and it will likely stay with us for the summer. However you look at it, our Saturday lunch was a spectacular event, with the warblers, the house wren, the catbird—and don't forget the old faithfuls of robins, blue jays, chickadees, tufted titmice, and cardinals, as well as ceaseless chatter of the gray squirrels.

Do you doubt that summer has arrived? If yes, Saturday evening clinched it. Jeremy had put up the hummingbird feeder a week or so ago. It goes on the same nail in the maple tree as the now removed winter seed feeder. And, during supper, our first hummingbird of the year visited. We have just the one species, the ruby-throated. He hovered with wings vibrating, inserted his needle-like beak into the narrow orifice of the bright-red plastic flower, drank, and in a flash he was gone. It is little short of an annual miracle that these hummingbirds, barely larger than a hawk moth, travel back and forth between the extreme southern tip of Mexico, Guatemala and Honduras to us and indeed into Canada. We look forward to many more hummingbird visitations, both to our artificial feeder and, once they are in flower, to the bright-red tubular flowers of our bee balm.

May 24, 2020

CHIPMUNKS AND WOODCHUCKS

This week I am writing mostly about two mammals that visit our backyard in the summer: the chipmunk and the woodchuck. But I will start at the beginning, when I arrived in the US in August 2008.

A high priority at the beginning was to get our newly purchased house repainted before the first winter. Peeling paint means rotting wood, means $$$. A single plank at the front got waterlogged one winter, and it really cost us to replace it. A friend of a friend recommended a painter, and we were all set. But it was a bumpy start. I emailed him the day before we agreed that he'd start to say I would be at home when he arrived in the morning. He replied he'd arrive at 4 p.m. OMG, this sounded like the start of a disaster! When he arrived at 4 p.m., he explained that he had a day job, 6 a.m. to 3 p.m., and that he'd be with me every day at 4 p.m. till nightfall. He kept his word, working at least six days a week, and he did a wonderful job. On the first day, he had his first OMG moment. At about 6 p.m., I asked him if he'd like a cup of tea. His jaw dropped (did I say a cup of arsenic?), but he swiftly regained his composure and explained slowly and deliberately, as if I had an IQ of 20, that he had plenty of cans of soda in the icebox at the back of his pickup (meaning pickup truck). I was climbing clumsily onto the bottom rung of the learning curve, including the gargantuan work ethic in the US. Over the weeks, the painter explained many all-American things to me, and I can't thank him enough! But one thing that he told me was very puzzling. He told me that the east fence, newly erected by our neighbors to keep the deer out and their small children in, was the wrong way round. The struts, three horizontals running the length of the fence and a vertical every six feet or so, should face inward to their backyard, not outward to ours. I couldn't understand why this was a problem. Soon I discovered that we are the lucky ones, on the right side of the fence for the Summer Chipmunk Show.

Our chipmunks use the horizontal struts of the east fence as runways. Time and again, we see a chipmunk run along the strut, pause for a microsecond, then squeeze through the narrow space between a vertical strut and the fence, make another six-foot dash to the next vertical strut, and so on. In this way, a chipmunk can get from one end of the backyard to the other, safe from the cat, the hawk, and the raccoon. We enjoy the chipmunk show on the fence so much.

In the summer—and it is now seriously summertime—the chipmunks are always busy. As well as on the fence, a chipmunk is often skittering around on our driveway, rushing in and out of the forsythia, occasionally pattering around on the deck, and then nosediving down under the garage door.

Chipmunks are everywhere. They live in backyards and parks, and especially in the forest, where they run around in the leaf litter and onto fallen logs. Altogether, chipmunks tend to stay on or near the ground, perhaps close to one of the many entrances to the complicated burrows they dig into sloping ground. Our chipmunks almost certainly use the bank between the garage and the fence, which we leave completely undisturbed. But this year, we

have a high-flyer chipmunk, often running over the steeply sloping garage roof onto the top of the south fence (without any use-
ful horizontal struts) and then to the lower branches of the black
walnut tree. But it has never ventured really high and lacks the
gymnastic skills of the squirrels.

Many of our fellow citizens love the chipmunks as much as we
do. Chipmunks exude an endless busyness and sheer enjoyment
of being alive. Always something to do, even if the activity sometimes appears to be totally pointless. When a chipmunk discovers
a bunch of goodies, whether berries or acorns, it crams them into
its hamster-like cheeks and heads swiftly for home. We occasionally see "a chipmunk with mumps" at this time of year, and routinely in the fall when chipmunks provision their burrows, so that
there is a quick snack at hand when they wake up during the long
winter hibernation.

Another reason why we can love chipmunks is that they don't
do any real damage. That cannot be said for the woodchuck. I have
mixed feelings about woodchucks. It feels so special to have a mar-
mot in our neighborhood, nearly two feet long, lumbering around
on the ground and occasionally standing up on its back legs to survey the scene. But I am glad that, somehow, we only have visiting
woodchucks and no resident. The other year, a woodchuck family
made its home under the porch (meaning front veranda) of a student house on the way to work. It was lovely to watch the family of
five woodchuck pups playing as I walked past in the early morning.
But as the woodchuck burrow extended through the summer, the
porch got more and more lopsided and even the left side of the house
started to lean. And the vegetation nearby was cropped right down,
unlike the usual overgrown jungle surrounding student houses.

We've had at least one woodchuck visitation to our yard this
year. The woodchuck sidled onto the low wall where our meadow

violets had flowered in the early spring (March 22), and then proceeded to munch all the violet leaves. I was steaming mad. Directly after "the enemy" had left, I sprayed everything with the bad egg spray. It was quite a stink! Yes, the woodchucks are wonderful, but so are our meadow violets.

Two other things are worth a mention this week. First, we have been enjoying watching our cottontail rabbit, who visits most days to feast on the dandelion and clover growing luxuriantly on our back lawn. But the meadow violets on the back lawn (which flower later than the violets on the east wall; see May 3) have set seed, and the grass has been growing so vigorously that Jeremy has been worrying about whether the lawnmower blades and his biceps will cope. The first mow of the year happened yesterday. Our rabbit will be cross. He may even abandon us. We shall see.

Second, a pair of robins decided to nest in our crab apple tree. It has been fun to watch, but their nest seemed rather exposed to the elements above. The robin nest building was also attracting the attention of the blue jays coming in from above and the squirrels coming up from below. It was all becoming a very noisy business. And then, suddenly on Thursday, the robins had abandoned the nest and it was quiet. As Jeremy mowed yesterday, he discovered eggshell. Nature had been red in tooth and claw, courtesy of one or other of the blue jays or gray squirrels.

May 31, 2020

LOOKING UP

I've decided to look up this week. That is easy to do from the deck, where we now have our breakfast and lunch on most days. We look up into the maple tree with rapidly expanding leaves that give us shade from the sun. Often, the catbird is there, singing its endlessly complicated songs; occasionally a hummingbird visits our feeder; and the gray squirrels hang precariously from the very tips of twigs to consume every new maple seed they can reach. But for the evening meal, we retreat indoors behind insect-proof screens on every window and the deck door. Although Jeremy is largely unaffected, I would be eaten alive unless smothered in DEET—and I am prepared to do that (with a heavy sigh) only when invited to the occasional evening barbecue.

Looking up farther, we see that—at long last—the black walnut at the southern end of the backyard has come in leaf. It is always the last. We are through those couple of weeks of May when the surrounding maples, ash, box elder, and more are all luscious green, while the tall black walnut remains bleakly wintry. Now, we have both plenty of black walnut foliage and bright-green catkins dangling from every branch. By September, there will be equally bright-green walnuts, the size of ping-pong balls—but don't linger or park your car under a black walnut tree at that time of year because a walnut fruit falling from the top of a tree can give you a mighty headache or dent your car roof. Altogether, they are very different from the walnut trees in the UK, much beloved of National Trust properties and Oxford college gardens. That walnut tree is called "English walnut" here, even though it is from Central Asia and is as much a cultivated tree in England as in the US.

The black walnut tree is native, and it is very common here. We are close to the northern limit of its range; just a little farther north, the frost-free growing season is too short for the fruits to ripen. The black walnut is mostly self-seeding, amply helped by squirrels, which love to carry the fruits around, bury them, and then forget about them. But black walnut is also harvested for very beautiful wood, on display in every craft shop and farmers' market hereabouts. You can find recipes for black walnut pie, too, but don't be taken in. Apparently it is a pain to get to the nut. A friend told me that the easiest way is to put your snow chains onto your car tires and drive back and forth over a line of fruits. (This seems like overkill to me, but the story makes the point.) You can buy the extracted nuts at great expense from the local organic food store but I am told that they are an acquired taste. So let's stay with buying what are quaintly called English walnuts, and leave the black walnuts to the squirrels.

There is yet another way that our black walnut tree figures large in our backyard. I have a much-thumbed printout of black walnut–compatible plants. Neglect the checklist and you will have dead (plant) bodies on your hands. Just as with other walnuts, the black walnut produces copious amounts of juglone, a complicated naphthalene molecule (sort of related to the active ingredient of mothballs), which inhibits respiratory enzymes. The standard story is that native plants that co-occur in the forests are fine, but that non-natives, like tulips, apple trees, and potatoes, are dead meat. Consistent with that, our redbud and hemlock trees are growing vigorously under the black walnut. But it really isn't so simple. Spicebush is supposed to be tolerant, but I am sure that our spicebush was miserable until we transplanted it away from the black walnut (see April 19) because it had chronic juglone poisoning. And the garlic mustard and greater celandine, both highly invasive imports from you-know-where, are undeterred by the juglone. But I am starting to look down, and that is a digression from this week's theme of looking up.

So, let us look even farther up, into the sky. On Friday afternoon, the weather gods were in a frenzy of thunder and torrential rain. Apart from that, the sky has been brilliant blue from horizon to horizon most days this week, or with patches of cumulus cloud. And on several days we have seen and heard the chimney swifts that visit us every summer. Wipe the standard image of a British swift from your mind. Forget the screams and the forked tail. The chimney swifts twitter discreetly and have a stubby tail, with all the elegance of "a cigar with wings" (standard bird book identification aid). And, yes, chimney swifts nest in chimneys. They need old-fashioned chimneys with wide flues, and the Cornell Lab of Ornithology has expressed concern that chimney swift numbers are declining as these old chimneys are being replaced by modern, narrow-flued chimneys. But in the US, there is a solution to every problem. You can buy a special twelve-foot-high chimney swift tower that you can assemble in your backyard. The picture on the website has a commercial digger in the background, suggesting that it may be a little more complex to assemble than an IKEA bookcase. Probably not a great idea for our small backyard. We can just enjoy our flying cigars twittering as they skim very high above our heads.

We have seen two other species of birds high overhead in the last week. On a couple of occasions, Canada geese have flown over, honking as they go. And the turkey vultures are with us in force, circling around, enjoying whatever thermals they can tap into. For other big birds, especially the osprey and the bald eagle, we will have to venture farther afield from our backyard to the shores of our nearest Finger Lake, Cayuga Lake.

June 7, 2020

NATIVES AND ALIENS

We have many uninvited guests in our backyard, and most are very welcome. Some are natives and they seem very exotic to us. Others are exotics, aka aliens or invasives. The exotics from Asia are also exotic for us, and the exotics from Europe are reassuringly familiar.

We are particularly enjoying two natives. One is the Virginia waterleaf, which has appeared quite suddenly this year under the maple tree and privet hedge. It is a member of the small family Hydrophyllaceae, related to the borages, and the clusters of pretty white flowers with long stamens are much loved by the bumblebees. As the flowers age, they turn pink, and some are now even purple. We initially thought its name a bit strange. Waterleaf sounds like a pond plant. But the name refers to white spots on the leaves that the early colonists apparently imagined looked like water stains. I lack that kind of imagination. The waterleafs are all plants of woodland edges.

Our other native is bloodroot with the glorious Linnaean name of *Sanguinaria canadensis*. This is a bit of a cheat because it is an invited guest derived from some rootstock kindly given to us by a friend. But it is very much an Ithacan habit to fill the yard with native plants. Altogether, bloodroot is a very strange plant.

It produces perfectly white but short-lived flowers, each at the apex of a stem wrapped in a leaf. When the flower is over, the leaf extends, becoming a large dark green plate. And why is it called bloodroot? Well, Anna Comstock has a lovely entry for this plant in her *Handbook of Nature Study* (1911): "Once in clearing a path through a woodland, we happened to hack off a mass of these root-stocks, and we stood aghast at the gory results." Just imagine her, in her long skirts, hat with a hatpin, and, presumably, a machete. How I wish I had known her! But getting back to bloodroot again, its sap is bright red and sticky. The active ingredient, known as sanguinarine, is an alkaloid and seriously toxic. Although used sparingly in traditional medicines, it was also painted onto weapons of Native Americans, which must have been scary for the opposition. The other day, I read how a Dr. Pinkard made a lot of money from his cure-all Pinkard's Sanguinaria Compound, until the feds caught up with him (in 1931) and fined him a hefty $25. With its bioactive latex, the bloodroot is, unsurprisingly, a member of the poppy family, even though it looks nothing like standard poppies.

One of the alien plants in our backyard thrives under our maple tree. It is Morrow's honeysuckle, come all the way from Japan. It was brought to the US in the 1870s for gardens, and the rest is history along roadsides and old railways. In fact, our honeysuckle plants likely came from the bushes down the road, courtesy of the robins, who greatly enjoy the bright-red berries. We have three plants that have been growing slowly but steadily for the last two or three years, and the largest of them has now produced flowers for the first time. They are so pretty, perfect honeysuckle flowers that start white and gradually turn yellow as they age. The robins and squirrels will enjoy the berries in the fall. But we need to keep an eye on this honeysuckle, as it can be aggressive and take over.

And then we have aliens that are, for us, reassuring familiars. Our mown lawn looks totally different from the meadow of last month (see May 24). Today's lawn has large clumps of white clover and black medick, and plenty of plantain leaves, with the first plantain flowers coming through. This year has brought a surprise for the front lawn, a lovely display of cat's ear that, alas, will be guillotined by Jeremy and the lawn mower this afternoon.

I am also tending our herb Robert, which is growing well under the black walnut at the south end of the backyard. Now, that does require some care because of a familiar but decidedly unwelcome guest from the UK, garlic mustard. I think of the days in the UK when we nurtured our small garlic mustard patch to attract orange-tip butterflies. I am entertained by these memories for most of the year, but I am not amused today! Garlic mustard is an invasive par excellence. Here in the US, it grows in luxurious thickets, and if I delay weeding it out until after flowering, the seeds ping everywhere, setting up for next year. I am not alone in my dislike of garlic mustard. It is officially a "Class-A Noxious Weed." Although we have European pierid white butterflies, the orange-tip never made it across the pond, and the swallowtails that we are starting to see in the yard won't touch it. I spent a cross, sweaty ten minutes digging out garlic mustard by the fistful yesterday afternoon, to give the herb Robert a chance, and that was just the start of this task. I need the fortitude of Anna Comstock.

June 14, 2002

SAVE THE BEES!

Everywhere we are being instructed to landscape and plant our backyards "for the bees." When I went to our local garden supplies shop this week to replenish our supply of bad egg deer spray, their whiteboard of Seasonal Tips was all about encouraging bees. Some of the tips are simple add-ins and others would require a degree in engineering. Time for a guilt trip. We do nothing but enjoy our bee guests that work our flowers. Just at present, we have on offer bee-friendly flowers of the so-called Russian sage (which isn't a sage and comes from Afghanistan and Iran, not Russia), lamb's ear also from Iran and thereabouts, and two uninvited guests, comfrey and white clover from the UK.

The honeybees are busy. But they are something of a mystery because we don't know where they are coming from. As far as we know, there are no hives nearby—probably the nearest are at the Cornell bee lab, which is a good three miles away. We really shouldn't be expecting those honeybees, especially as they have many sweet treats much closer to hand. Until recently, the bees could have come from the Cornell Orchards, which at 1.5 miles is a long but not crazy commute for a foraging honeybee. But Cornell Orchards threw out their hives five years ago, and they are now totally dependent on wild bees with no reduction in yield of their apples, pears, and more. Is it possible that our honeybees may come from feral nests in the scraps of woodland within a half-mile radius of our house where the deer hang out? Feral colonies of honeybees are much more abundant here than in the UK because many of the European settlers failed to manage the bees that they brought with them, and some wild colonies have been so for centuries, dating back even to the 1600s. Many of the feral bees are believed to have come from East Europe and West Asia, and they are more tolerant of our cold winters than the strains of *Apis mellifera mellifera* brought from mild, wet England.

We also have many bumblebees. Most of them are the native *Bombus impatiens* (the common eastern bumblebee) with a yellow, furry thorax and black abdomen. The bees at the comfrey today are noticeably smaller than the bumblebees at our bugle a month ago, and that's because only the workers are foraging now. The queens, who were foraging in the spring, are in their nests, which they have constructed in discarded chipmunk burrows and other holes in the ground. Each queen is busy making eggs, having persuaded her first offspring to do all the work, including collecting pollen and nectar. It is only later in the season that we will see queens again, and these will be new queens out briefly before they hibernate for the winter. I am glad that the bumblebees in our yard are truly wild. Many are not. Just like honeybees, bumblebees are bundled up and transported back and forth across the continent to pollinate this crop here and then that crop there. The Big Scandal everyone hears about is the trucking of vast numbers of honeybees in February to California for the almond crop (Google tells me it is 420 million bees), but our local commercial apiaries rarely indulge in that money-spinner because their bees, taken abruptly from midwinter to balmy California, do the job badly. Instead, commercially reared bumblebees, both native and introduced species, are big business as pollinators, especially for local tomato growers.

But I am not an enthusiast for all bees. I was reminded of this when an enormous carpenter bee blundered into me during my run earlier this week, a bull's-eye straight to the forehead. I don't think there are carpenter bees in the UK. Carpenter bees do as their name suggests. They chew out wood to make a nest in the twigs or branches of trees—and in wooden houses. The bee that bumped into me was the aptly named large carpenter bee, *Xylocarpa virginica*, a big and almost square beast with a very shiny black abdomen and dark wings. These bees career around, always flying fast but looking unbalanced as if they are about to topple midair.

A few years ago, one oh-so-smart carpenter bee queen decided that the front of our garage would be the perfect place to raise her brood. Before we knew where we were, we had a gaping hole and an ugly stream of brown frass running down the front of our recently repainted white garage. By the end of the season, she had succumbed to whatever, and her happy brood had found comfortable hidey-holes to hibernate in before they eyed up our house and garage the following year. Then, in late fall, the pileated woodpecker visited, spotted the hole, decided that there must be something tasty in there, and gouged out a much bigger hole, littering the driveway with big fragments of wood from our garage. Next spring, we replaced the planking and repainted.

Now, every year I check the house and garage for carpenter bee activity. I am happy to give the large carpenter bee full visitor rights, but please go nest somewhere else.

June 21, 2020

A TERMINOLOGICAL JUNGLE

It is midsummer, and our backyard is framed in green. That bright hard green of fully expanded tree leaves all the way up to the brilliant blue sky and hot summer sun. It is the time for sun hats, shorts, and perspiration. No complaints—it is good to feel warm to the bones. And it is also the time to brush up on our US tree identification, made simpler by the mature leaves on full display. But "brushing up" is a euphemism. As we turn to our increasingly battered bible, *The Sibley Guide to Trees* (Sibley 2009), for help and inspiration, we know that this season's work involves both relearning our achievements of last year and taking a few more faltering steps into the world of American trees. Our half-century with the British oak, ash, birch, and sycamore was no preparation for this. Even the little guide to trees of New York, which includes only the obvious and common species, has five species of birch, six of ash, nine of maple (same genus as the sycamore in Britain), and eleven oak species. And this genuine biological complexity is compounded by a near-limitless terminological jungle.

Let's start with the wonderful maple just next to our deck. We have identified our maple as a red maple, *Acer rubrum* (see May 10), because its perfectly maple-shaped leaves are rather small (smaller than the sugar maple leaf on the Canada flag), and it has the telltale bright red flowers of a red maple in the early spring. But the superbly well-informed tree man who has come to trim our maple calls it a silver maple because the overall form of the tree is highly branched and many of the branches are horizontal or even drooping, apparently fail-safe identifiers for a silver maple. We also have to admit that the bark is peeling away in funny strips, just like the silver maples farther down the road. But the leaves on the silver maples are different; they look as though a small child has attacked the flag maple leaf with blunt scissors. However hard we try, our maple ain't no silver maple. But there is a way out of this conundrum. Apparently the two species hybridize, and the hybrids are called "Freeman" maples. And then the hybrids cross with each other and with the parental species, and we have a host of trees that are more or less like the red or silver species. Our tree could be a Freeman that is closer to the red than to the silver species. Perhaps we should just let other people apply names as they see fit.

Another terminological muddle is in our eastern neighbor's backyard. It sort of belongs in our backyard too because it is right up against the fence and it gives me welcome shade on my daily run along the drive. It is a box elder. But don't be taken in. It is neither a box nor an elder. It is another of the nine common maple tree species here in New York, *Acer negundo* to be precise. This is a totally crazy tree, with leaves like an ash, not a maple at all. Apparently, you can always tell that a box elder is a maple, and none of the six local ash species, because its leaflets are irregularly toothed. But am I really sure that I understand what irregular teeth look like?

Dear Reader, are you getting a headache? Welcome to the world of US trees. This is not a world for wimps.

Up until yesterday evening, we had an even crazier problem of nomenclature in front of the house. A sycamore! No, not the sycamore maple, *Acer pseudoplatanus,* that is so abundant in the UK. This sycamore has crossed the pond and does well on Cape Cod and Long Island but it doesn't cope with the Ithacan winters. No, the sycamore is the American sycamore, *Platanus occidentalis,* a relative of the London plane tree. (If you want to get into the weeds with this, the London plane tree is actually a hybrid between the American and Oriental species, probably arising from an accidental crossing in Spain in the seventeenth century.) Getting back to the American sycamore, we often see it in damp woodland, and it is occasionally planted as a street tree in Ithaca. Our fellow citizens call their plane tree a sycamore because it is in the "sycamore" family (Platanaceae, which Brits call the plane tree family), unlike Brit-style sycamores, which are in the Aceraceae (meaning the maples). Got that?

This word game ends with some real activity. We had a self-sown *Platanus occidentalis* sapling growing in the front, within six inches of the house, but alas, it was getting too big. Jeremy got out a spade yesterday evening and our sycamore/plane tree is no more.

June 28, 2020

EMPIRES UNDER THE MAPLE TREE

Everything in the backyard has changed very rapidly over the first half of summer. Today, as I look under the maple tree, there is a near-monoculture of lily of the valley leaves. We planted a few bulbs about eight years ago, and it has spread gloriously. But it was a rather poor display of flowers this year, and perhaps we should thin them out a bit at the end of the summer. You could not have imagined this "under the maple tree empire of lily of the valley" just six to ten weeks ago, when this space was the kingdom of lesser celandines, along with a few brave hairy bittercress and the ubiquitous ground ivy. Now, there is no sign of the celandines above ground. Their leaves shriveled and simply disappeared over the first couple of weeks of June heat, and their bulbils, swollen with nutrients, will lie low just below the soil surface until next April. By late May, with swiftly rising temperatures, the world of lesser celandines was replaced by a sea of blue forget-me-nots for a full two weeks before being taken over by today's world of lily of the valley.

But the forget-me-nots did not disappear by themselves. After seed set, the stem skeletons remained, increasingly colonized by fungi. So the other day, I put on my gardening gloves and took them out from among the lily of the valley plants. It was very easy, and they came out, dying roots and all, without the aid of the trowel, spilling seed for next year back to the earth. A thoroughly good Sunday afternoon's work, I thought.

My views on all of that had changed dramatically by Tuesday morning. I woke with my right forearm covered in a swollen rash that was furiously itchy but too painful to scratch. Yup, it was poison ivy! We checked out under the maple tree, and, yes, there was a telltale leaf ("leaves of three, let them be" and all that). Poison ivy is the nettle of North America. Of course, it is a different plant altogether from the nettle; it is a sumac that goes, appropriately enough, by the name *Toxicodendron radicans*. And poison ivy is a whole lot sneakier than nettles. For a start, you don't know that you are in trouble until a day or so after coming into contact with it. The toxin is called urushiol and it is in the sap, released when the plant is damaged. (If you remember your organic chemistry, urushiol is actually a catechol, and its effect can be more or less severe, depending on the exact composition of the hydrocarbon side chain.) The other sneaky problem is that it is a very variable plant, and more mental effort is needed to identify poison ivy than a nettle. It can creep along the ground, it can climb on trees and posts, and it can even form a shrub. (I've not seen that, and Heaven forbid!) In fact, it was first called poison ivy by the colonists of the 1600s because of the way it clings to trees with lots of little aerial roots, just like real ivy. That's why its specific name is *radicans*, meaning rootlets.

So, suddenly the world under the maple tree had changed again, this time into a battleground. I needed the Full Poison Ivy Gear. I donned a long-sleeved shirt, together with long pants and rubber boots (translation: trousers and Wellingtons), and then I tucked the shirt under the cuffs of thick disposable gloves, which happen to be in a delicate shade of bright purple. Finally, I took a plastic bag that, contrary to the spirit of state law, was definitely not going to be reused, and I ventured into the tangled bank under the maple tree. Perspiring profusely with all this gear in the heat, I tracked from the leaf to the ground, loosened the soil with the trowel, and then yanked. Up came not just this one plantlet but five feet of the stuff that had been hidden under all the other vegetation. I stuffed it into the bag, tied the bag tightly, and put it into the household garbage. Then I washed my hands and arms in a ridiculous frenzy for more than a minute. I fear that there is still poison ivy lurking under the maple tree, but that was enough for one day and the rest will have to be dealt with another time.

Despite the Poison Ivy Trauma, there is much under the maple tree that gives us great pleasure. The Virginia waterleaf is now over, and it has been replaced by two more lovely native species, the daisy fleabane and white avens. The daisy fleabane is just what the name suggests, clusters of small daisy-like flowers at the tips of a branching plant, anywhere from two to four feet tall. We have it all over the yard, and we tend it with loving care. The white avens is a newcomer to our backyard and also well named: just like the British wood avens, but with pretty white flowers. Incidentally, we also have yellow avens, which—with its yellow flowers—is even more like wood avens. We initially misidentified yellow avens as wood avens but, checking more carefully, we find that wood avens hasn't crossed the pond.

I will just finish off with a PS to my diary entry of two weeks ago about bees (see June 14). I mentioned then about how we guiltily neglect repeated instructions on all the things we should do to "save the bees." A few days after writing about this, I received an email from a colleague with "online resources" about how to make our lawn a bee lawn. We are instructed to plant our lawn with white clover, selfheal, dandelion, and creeping Charlie. But we have three out of four without even trying! So, I googled creeping Charlie to work out how we are deficient. I laughed out loud: creeping Charlie is a US name for ground ivy. We have enough of that to feed every bee in Ithaca. So we can now hold our heads high and tell the world that we have a perfect bee lawn. Perhaps best left unsaid is that this has been achieved by benign neglect because the downside of the amazing work ethic in this country is that many of our fellow citizens would disapprove of such effortless achievement. As importantly, our cottontail has forgiven us for mowing the lawn, and he visits our newly named Bee Lawn almost every evening for his last and lengthy meal of the day.

July 5, 2020

FIREFLIES: A WONDER OF
THE ITHACA WORLD

We are now in the time of the greatest Wonder of the Ithaca World. Yes, the fireflies have come out. A quick wander round the backyard as it gets dark—about 9 p.m. (we are at a much lower latitude than the UK, closer to Madrid)—and there they are. Flashes of light high up in the maple and black walnut trees, in the shadow of the redbud and the privet hedge, and close to the ground, especially on the lawn. Then, more flashing lights on the front lawn, and in everyone else's yard up and down the street. It is a mesmerizing sea of dancing lights.

But fireflies aren't flies. They are beetles of the family Lampyridae. Their flashes come from the last three segments of their abdomen. In other words, the tail end of the beetle has been transformed into a lantern. Making light needs a lot of oxygen, and the beetles make each and every flash by releasing a tiny pulse of oxygen. And they have to get those oxygen puffs at precisely the right frequency because the light flash is a mating signal. I watch them with pure wonder, remembering how I struggle to get the tempo even halfway right in my faltering attempts to play the piano. Back to the fireflies, the males cruise around, flashing at the right tempo for their species, while the females sit on the ground and watch the display. If a female sees a flash sequence she likes, she flashes back, again at just the right frequency. Then the male descends and, following a few further flashy rechecks, they mate. In due course, the female will lay her eggs on damp soil. The larvae are fierce predators in leaf litter and soil, taking two years to reach adulthood.

We haven't worked out the firefly species at all. There are supposedly twenty species in our area, each with its own special sequence of flashes. We think that we mostly have *Photinus pyralis*, the common eastern firefly, which is said to be particularly common in gardens and flashes in yellow (some other species go for green), but who knows. We may also have some cheat species that lie low, flash like the female of their victim species, and then gobble up the amorous male. The world of the fireflies is not a gentle world.

As we watched our firefly display yesterday evening, we suddenly noticed we were not alone. There was our cottontail rabbit sitting in the middle of the lawn, very upright, with his ears aloft, absolutely still, and totally unperturbed by us. And far above the firefly display, the stars were shining in the perfectly cloudless sky. Then, crash-bang, again and again. Yes, it was the Fourth of July, and time for fireworks. We sighed a heavy sigh at the stupidity of humans. Who could possibly need fireworks when there are fireflies, a cottontail, and a sky full of stars?

It feels so special for fireflies to be everywhere, compared to just a single, rather rare species in the UK. They weren't always so rare. After all, they were so commonplace that Thomas Hardy used them as a backdrop for that astonishing gambling event in *The Return of the Native* (Hardy [1878] 1985): "As their eyes grew accustomed to the darkness, they perceived faint greenish points of light among the grass and fern. These lights dotted the hillside like stars of a low magnitude. 'Ah, glowworms,' said Wildeve. 'Wait a minute. We can continue the game.' Venn sat still, and his companion went hither and thither till he had gathered thirteen glowworms—as many as he could find in a space of four or five minutes." Kind of easier to do with the British firefly *Lampyris noctiluca* because the female has no wings and looks like the larva (hence the term glowworm). Apparently, the females of some firefly species here would also qualify as glowworms (although I haven't heard people here refer to fireflies as glowworms). Females of our common species *Photinus pyralis* are proper adult beetles with wings, but it seems they rarely fly.

The fireflies are our fun beetles of July. But we have another beetle that is a misery, the Japanese beetle, *Popillia japonica*. It is a big, ugly scarab beetle with a lurid green thorax and shiny brown forewings covering the abdomen—and it eats. It can munch its way through any leaf, leaving just the leaf veins. A Japanese beetle party (yes, they love to hang out together) can reduce a plant to a stem supporting leaf skeletons. As the name suggests, this beetle came from Japan many years ago, and it has munched its way through the Northeast and Midwest ever since. It was exactly a century ago, in 1920, that attempts to eradicate it were abandoned and defeat was admitted. Although we see the adults only in July and August, the Japanese beetle is with us the year round because the larvae live underground and eat the roots of grass and other plants. A bad infestation can destroy the garden lawn. But I do not admit defeat. In late June of each year, I buy a Japanese beetle trap at the local garden supplies shop, and I hang it on the washing line. It has a slow-emission pad of the sex pheromone, together with some friendly leaf scents, positioned above a green plastic bag to collect all the beetles that fly in. It is wonderfully simple and very specific. When I take the trap down at the end of the season, the haul is almost entirely Japanese beetle. It really works. As I put the washing out on Saturday morning, two of these ugly beasts flew into the trap and tumbled down to their doom.

July 12, 2020

THE DEPTFORD PINK

Nowadays, I have to watch my step as I go to the washing line in the backyard. This is because I am walking through the Empire of the Deptford Pink. This empire flourishes every year in July, and it is particularly vigorous this year with some two dozen plants. At the top of each stem there is a cluster of flowers, each with five bright pink petals laid out perfectly flat, as if to soak in the sun of high summer in its adopted land.

The Deptford pink is our most cherished invasive. Why, over and above all those other reassuringly familiar invasives from Britain? The answer is simple. The Deptford pink is rare in the UK, so rare that we had never knowingly seen it, but here it is—thriving uninvited and magnifico in our backyard. The Deptford pink is a sad business in Britain, as two sources in our bookcase remind us. The first source is David McClintock and Richard Fitter's 1956 *Collins Pocket Guide to Wild Flowers*—of Britain, of course, but it is such a classic that there is no need to include that in the title (McClintock and Fitter 1956). At that time, the Deptford pink was described as widespread but scarce, being restricted to dry, grassy spots. And our second source is Richard Mabey's *Flora Britannica* from 1996, by which time the status of the Deptford pink was decidedly rare (Mabey 1996). So, no need to slow down and scan the roadside when you next visit Deptford in London because you'd be as likely to see a bald eagle as a Deptford pink. Indeed, Mabey declares that Deptford pinks have never inhabited Deptford. How come? This beautiful little plant was named in Gerard's *Herball* of 1633, but Gerard got his pinks muddled (easy to do, let's be honest). From the description, it appears that he had seen a different species, the maiden pink, somewhere near Deptford and somehow conflated these maiden pinks with the real McCoy Deptford pink, which was only ever found in the countryside. Of course, the maiden pink is now as rare and threatened as the Deptford pink in the UK.

The really wonderful thing about our Deptford pinks is that their empire in our backyard is not so very special. The Deptford pink is widespread in fields and on the side of roads (and probably in everyone's backyards if only they didn't mow their lawns so often). Now that it is thriving, it ignores all that stiff upper lip stuff in British field guides about needing dry, sandy conditions to survive. For example, we saw flourishing Deptford pinks just next to a wet, muddy rut, when walking in some rough cattle pasture in the Finger Lakes National Forest yesterday.

The Deptford pink is not the only success story in the US. The other very obvious success stories of this week are the strawberries. I don't mean the big red blobs created in the 1700s in France by crossing two wild species (one is the native wild species in the US and other from Chile). You can find the big red blobs in plastic containers all year round in our grocery store, brought all the way from the Central Valley (California) or Mexico in refrigerated trucks (translation: stonking great lorries). Our backyard is delightfully different, with the British wild strawberry, misnamed here as wood strawberry, and the Indian strawberry, also misnamed because it comes from China. Now in July, the wild strawberry runners are spreading fast under the maple tree. The pretty white flowers are long past, replaced by lots of perfect, miniature, bright-red strawberry fruits. The Indian strawberry has set up on the other side of the deck, in the bed under the kitchen window. Look low, beneath the bee balm and the Russian sage plants, and there it is, the leaves carpeting the surface and its delicate yellow flowers of May replaced by another army of tiny bright-red fruits.

The wild strawberry tastes great, but we don't know about the Indian strawberry; there seems to be a vigorous Internet debate about whether the Indian strawberry tastes like watermelon, is tasteless (the same thing according to my taste buds), or is distasteful. Whatever, we do not harvest these gloriously colorful fruits for our dining table. Instead, we leave these uninvited guests for the delight of uninvited diners. Until a few days ago, I had assumed that our strawberries were enjoyed only by the chipmunks, squirrels, and occasional robin (that's a thrush, remember). But it has been twice recently that I have spotted a shrew, the northern short-tailed shrew—*Blarina brevicauda* to be precise—near the Indian strawberry patch. The first time, it scampered across the driveway from the strawberries to a hole under the wall, straight in front of me as I was running, and the second time it was busy under the bee balm. Of course, it could have been feasting on earthworms or slugs. (It is reported to eat salamanders, mice, and birds, too, but I don't think they are on the menu under the bee balm.) But apparently *Blarina* also like berries, and what could be a better snack than a few thriving invasive strawberries?

July 19, 2020

BLUE JAY BIRDS AND BLUE JAY HUMANS

The songsters of the early summer have fallen silent. Nowadays, there is no catbird to serenade our breakfast and lunch on the deck, no tufted titmouse calling "Peee-ter, Peee-ter" from the maple tree, and no buzz of grace notes from a Carolina wren in the privet hedge. Occasionally we hear a faint catbird mew (it's not called a catbird for nothing), and even the early morning robin is desultory. They are far too busy making more catbirds, tufted titmice, Carolina wrens, and robins, all exhausted by the rigors of parenting in the heat.

So, what do we hear in our backyard today? Blue jays galore. Everything done by a blue jay has to be commented on in real time and in great detail. Whether the blue jay is on its own or in a gang, whether at rest on a branch of the black walnut or flying from the box elder to the maple, there is the endless clamor of jay screams, each one telling the world that "I am here" and "this is how I feel" about life. Add to this the kuk-kuk and teeth chattering of the gray squirrels and the shrill chirp-chirp-chirp (going on for five or ten minutes in perfect time) of the chipmunk. Altogether, it is the perfect backyard cacophony of mid-July.

But this summer is different. We have another mammal contributing to the din. Our neighbors on the east side are doing a major renovation of their house. As they leave their house vacant for the remodeling, we are invaded by a gang of workmen who are as melodious and introverted as the blue jays. We sneak out onto the deck, thinking, "Aha, this time, all is quiet on the eastern front." Then, as we crunch into the first radish of a lunchtime salad, there is a hoot of laughter or howl of anguish, followed by loud and long explanation. Or we take an early morning sip of breakfast coffee, congratulating ourselves on beating them to it . . . and, as if from nowhere, there comes a hollering between the upstairs window and the backyard as they tell one another the exciting, often expletive-laden events since they were last together the previous afternoon. They are mostly cheerful and get on with the job but, inescapably, they are blue jays in human form. And of course, being American humans means that they have all sorts of noisy equipment as accompaniment. How about some reverberating hammering, the friendly squeal of an electric drill, or record-breaking decibels of an unbalanced electric saw? When they started, they clocked off mid-afternoon. But the owner came back briefly, and now they keep going till our afternoon teatime at 4 pm, and beyond.

But there might be compensations. All this disruption seems to have deterred the black cat that terrorized our chipmunks earlier in the year. Jeremy has muttered dark things about cats and cars on the nearby main road, but I distinctly saw the black cat last week loitering with intent near one of the houses on the other side of our road. Also, we haven't had a visitation from the woodchuck in several weeks (see May 24), and our meadow violet leaves on the wall are recovering—although I am keeping up the bad egg spray just in case.

The other compensation is that the weekends are a haven of peace. But as we sat down to breakfast on Saturday morning, confident of some quiet solitude, there was suddenly a terrible commotion in the box elder. The decibels of the electric saw were nothing compared to this. Then, out flew a blue jay to the maple tree above us, with a furious male robin hard on its heels. They landed about our heads, screaming at each other. Then another blue jay flew in from the other end of the backyard, presumably to join the fun. The first jay, perhaps a trifle ruffled by the situation, decided this was a good moment to make its exit, leaving its pal to finish the altercation. In due course, the weary robin flew back to the box elder, we hope to find his family intact. After all, the blue jay is a merciless predator of the eggs and nestlings of other birds.

This morning's breakfast, I am pleased to report, was tranquil. But some things in the backyard just carry on through all this racket. I should mention one thing in particular because it will be old news after this week. It is the daylilies. We have a patch of them next to the forsythia, glorious apricot-orange lily flowers. Each flower is with us for just one day, and—all things being equal—there is a steady parade of five or six flowers each day over a period of about three weeks. Daylilies, or *Hemerocallis fulva* for the purists, have an entry in our wildflower guide to the US Northeast because, although they are garden plants from Japan and China, they have escaped big-time. Whether you love or hate this invasive alien, it provides a splash of color to roadside ditches and woodland edges in the countryside. In our backyard, we mostly leave the daylily patch to do its thing, but I do have to spray the buds, which seem to be a delicacy for the deer. One year, I saw a deer curl its lips back and, oh so delicately, snip off a head of buds with its incisors, and munch in evident enjoyment. Needless to say, I tore out into the yard, screaming like a blue jay, and the rest of the buds were saved on that occasion. We were not so lucky this year. On Friday we had enough buds for another week or so of daylily flowers. But a deer must have come in on Friday night. The terminal buds of every shoot had been excised with perfect precision. How was this possible when I spray with the bad egg spray every weekend? I can only imagine that, in the heat, the smell and taste of bad eggs had decayed very fast. Whatever the reason, our next backyard daylily flower will be in July 2021.

You must imagine that this is sufficient cacophony for one summer in Ithaca. But it is only the start. This last week, we heard our first scissor grinder cicada, *Tibicen pruinosa*. As our fireflies start to wane, the hubbub will soon be upon us. Watch this space . . .

July 26, 2020

CALL MY BLUFF

I have a vivid memory that my school biology textbook included a grainy black-and-white photograph of a perched bird with liquid streaming from its beak onto a crumpled wreck that was falling toward the bottom of the picture. The caption read something like: blue jay vomits after feeding on a monarch butterfly (presumably the crumpled wreck), which contains toxins stored from milkweed plants eaten by the caterpillar. I remember it so well because of my response on every occasion when I passed that page in the textbook. It was so exotic! After all, blue jays were as probable as blue swans; perhaps monarch butterflies were "brought out" for important royal occasions, like commemorative postage stamps; and there was no entry for milkweed in the index of the *Observer's Book of Wild Flowers*. (If you tut-tut me for not googling milkweed, you will be like the American tourist who tut-tutted about building Windsor Castle under the Heathrow fly pass.) Perfectly logically, I classified the exotic blue jay–monarch butterfly–milkweed story to the same fantasy world as the grainy black-and-white pictures of the Loch Ness Monster and the illustrated stories about Saint George's dragon and Perseus's Medusa.

Fast-forward half a century, and here I am in that fantasy world of ubiquitous blue jays in the trees and the occasional monarch butterfly flitting across our backyard. In this new world, the event in that ancient photograph is a trivial footnote to the big story. We are everywhere urged to "save our monarchs"—and that doesn't mean a certain beleaguered family with one residence in the market town of Windsor, Berkshire. We are bombarded with advice about how to protect these beautiful butterflies. The main solution advocated to every right-minded citizen is to grow milkweeds in their backyard. But monarchs are complicated creatures, more like migratory birds than other butterflies. Our monarchs have two winter residences, either at the southern tip of Florida or in the Sierra Madre mountains of Mexico. Although it is often claimed that the declines are caused by a dearth of milkweed food plants in the summer, some people doubt this and prefer to wring their hands about degradation of the overwintering sites and troubles during migration. Whatever the science, a patch of milkweed in your backyard is a badge of honor. Needless to say, I will sow some milkweed seeds next year.

But none of this matters to our new broods of blue jays. They have a lesson to learn. Their first meal of monarch butterfly will inevitably end in gastric disaster, courtesy of those cardiac glycosides from the milkweed, and each bird will, for evermore, associate the bright orange wings with black veins and fetching white spots with a stomachache from hell. But do spare a moment's thought for the sacrificial butterfly that taught this lesson.

Our backyard may be fantastically exotic, but it is still Darwinian. The Monarch Lesson provides the opportunity for a Pretender to the Throne, called the viceroy butterfly. The viceroy is not closely related to the monarch, but it looks just like a monarch, although a little smaller. Provided the blue jay (and other wannabe predators) have learned their lesson with a real McCoy monarch, the viceroy has a free pass to fly through our backyard and beyond without danger of molestation. So long as the viceroy doesn't get so common as to muddle the lesson, it can play the game of Call My Bluff with impunity.

A few days ago, we spotted another butterfly that plays Call My Bluff with the blue jays. It is the wonderful spicebush swallowtail, a full four inches across and with gloriously iridescent blue markings on its otherwise black wings. It was moseying about our spicebush, and we will find out before long if we have a happy brood of defoliating caterpillars. Like the viceroy, the spicebush swallowtail has a free pass vis-à-vis the blue jays. In this case, it is because it looks just like the pipevine swallowtail, which feeds on—you've guessed—pipevines, also known as Dutchman's pipe. The pipevine swallowtail stores a bunch of pipevine toxins, which are particularly nasty-looking four-ringed aromatic compounds generically called aristolochic acids. We are a little north of the natural range of Dutchman's pipe (*Aristolochia durior*), but people grow it as an ornamental vine, and there are plenty of escapes into natural habitats too. As I tell myself every year, I will be planting Dutchman's pipe alongside those milkweeds next spring.

I have just one more Call My Bluff story for this week. It involves us as well as blue jays, and there is no gastrointestinal distress. We were admiring some little metallic black bees (I think they are masked bees, probably species in the genus *Hylaeus*) on our cone flowers when I noticed some dirt on one of the petals. On this perfectly hot, still day, the dirt was moving. Goodness, but it was alive and it was rocking back and forth, attached to the petal at either end. We needed to do some homework on this fantastical beast. A quick Google search (how different from the days when I was stonewalled if it wasn't in the *Observer's Book of . . .*) and there it was as Caterpillar of the Week (October 7, 2015) of the online Caterpillar Lab. Our moving dirt is the camouflaged looper, *Synchlora aerata*, which will grow up to be a wavy-lined emerald moth. The caterpillar plays Call My Bluff by biting off bits of flower petal, bending its head downward to pat on a blob of sticky silk from its silk-making organs just beneath the mouth, and then arching back to stick the petal piece on its back. By the time we saw the camouflaged looper, it had covered itself in floral pieces that had faded to a very plausible aggregate of debris. If it hadn't behaved like a looper caterpillar, I'd have written it off as a bit of plant/soil litter. The Caterpillar Lab tells us that the camouflaged looper particularly likes composites, with daisy fleabane as a firm favorite. So, we are now on the lookout for gymnastic debris on the many daisy fleabanes that flourish in our backyard.

August 2, 2020

TERMITE MOUND OR ITALIAN VILLA?

This time last week it was seriously hot, and we were bracing ourselves for a blistering Monday morning in the high nineties before thunderstorms forecast in the early afternoon. We have two strategies for managing the heat. One is to become a termite mound in the savanna of sub-Saharan Africa. We open all the windows to create airflow that pulls the cool air up from our underground chamber (the basement). This works well for much of the summer, with the added benefit that we can see and hear what is going on outside when we are working indoors. But as the temperature outside rises, the airflow switches. Pure heat streams in through the windows and a wall of hot, still air sits at the top of the basement steps. The termite mound has collapsed, and we transition to a Mediterranean-style siesta in a country villa in Tuscany, with all windows and doors firmly shut and all curtains drawn. We sit it out in the gloom, divorced from the outside world. In principle, there is a third strategy. You could call it the Ithaca Strategy. It is to open the window wide and shove in a portable air conditioner. These contraptions are dressed-up refrigerator units, noisy, energy-guzzling, and relatively ineffective, despite the claims of Walmart and friends that they will solve all our problems. So far, we have not succumbed once to the third strategy. In principle, strategy three would be easy because the previous owners left their bulky AC units in one of the bedroom closets (aka walk-in cupboard: wardrobes aren't the done thing here). All we'd need to do is delve into the closet and haul them out from under the piles of discarded blankets.

So, what happens outside in the heat? Well, I can report on last Monday because, true to form, I went out in the midday sun for my pre-lunch run on the drive. No birds were evident, the marjoram on the east bank was starting to wilt, and the black-eyed Susans were drooping. The only thing to keep me company was a scissor grinder cicada occupying the honey locust tree in the front of the eastern neighbor's house. Again and again, the cicada buzzed long and loud. I can give you some numbers for that.

The scissor grinder cicada buzz lasts for about twenty seconds, and that is a good way to distinguish it from the other common cicada hereabouts, the Linne's cicada, which buzzes at a higher pitch and for just ten to fifteen seconds. It is tempting to compare this amazing insect to the soprano opera singer who can hold her note unbelievably long, but please don't be tempted. It, or rather he (because he is singing to attract the females), sings with his tymbals. On each side of his abdomen, there is a small patch of thin membrane, instead of the hard and crunchy skeleton that covers the rest of his body. The membrane is scored by many so-called ribs, each of a diameter less than the width of a human hair. A bunch of muscles vibrate the tymbal, forcing the ribs together—noisily!—and then pulling them apart—noisily!—about three hundred to four hundred times a second. So every pulse of song involves up to eight thousand vibrations, and he will keep at it, at least twice a minute, for hours and hours.

You need another number to understand the accompaniment to my run. These cicadas sing loud, a good one hundred decibels.

It is truly astonishing that a beast less than two inches long can be as loud as an opera singer in full bellow. This is achieved partly by timing the vibrations so that the sound waves from the two tymbals perfectly overlap. Also, the abdomen is full of air sacs, making a resonating chamber. Altogether, he is as loud as Maria Callas, while expending minimal amounts of energy. But the cicada is no Maria Callas. His song transports you not to La Scala opera house but to those few minutes at Newark Airport when you walk out to the commuter plane to Ithaca, right next to a monster transcontinental plane revving up for takeoff. Whatever you and I may think of all this, Mrs. Scissor Grinder can't claim that she never heard him call.

After my thirty minutes' run, I retreated from the Boeing 747 cicada to the comparative cool of indoors. The sky remained obstinately blue, with no sign of a thunderstorm. So we decided to transition from a savanna termite mound to a Tuscan villa. As we closed the dining room curtains, we noticed a single grackle on the lawn. This was odd because every grackle loves the company of other grackles. A solitary grackle is like a Philip Pullman character separated from its daemon. But even worse, the grackle was pacing up and down, with its beak wide open. We just hoped that this poor bird would come to its senses and retreat into the comparative cool under the forsythia, in the privet hedge, or in the canopy of the maple or black walnut.

It did rain eventually. The most humungous thunderstorms rolled in sometime in the middle of the night, and we reverted to a sub-Saharan termite mound for the rest of the week.

I will finish today with a brief postscript to last week's letter. On Thursday we spotted a female black swallowtail. She looks rather similar to the spicebush swallowtail, and she is also a Call My Bluff mimic of the toxic pipevine swallowtail. She was checking out our patch of wild carrot, and perhaps we will have the honor of hosting a late summer black swallowtail caterpillar. Our wild carrot is an uninvited guest to our backyard, and it is in full bloom. Despite its status as an invasive alien, we are delighted that the black swallowtail is in agreement with us that wild carrot is altogether very splendid.

August 9, 2020

HAPPY FAMILIES

A big storm slammed into the Carolinas last Tuesday and roared north, streaming inland directly over us to Canada, before petering out somewhere in northern Quebec. It caused mayhem just about everywhere it went, especially along the seaboard to New York and Connecticut, but we just had a cool day of solid, gusty rain. After it had gone, we cleared the drive and lawn of twigs and leaves torn from the trees in the wind, and we thanked our lucky stars that it was no worse than that for us. The ground soaked up the rain and even the brown patches on the lawn now look a little less frazzled. But for the birds, it was a time to hunker down out of harm's way, neglecting their normal activities for the day.

And the normal activities for the birds at this time of year can best be described as "busy, busy, busy." They have broods of offspring to get safely off their hands. Although that is most evident for the noisy blue jays, all the birds are at it. The robins, especially the male, pace the lawn for insects and worms, then fly off with a bill full of goodies. And those goodies became superabundant on the wet lawn post-Tuesday, as creatures escaped from drowning underground—into the tender beak of the robin. On several occasions, family groups of twittering chickadees have passed through our maple tree, and the crab apple and pin cherry in the front have been visited by the garrulous house sparrows from the bottom of the road, with a quiverful of youngsters in tow. I watched a tailless Carolina wren tumble about in the privet hedge. It was literally trying to find its feet, accompanied by increasingly vexed tweeting of a parent concealed nearby in the hedge. But undoubtedly the most attentive parents of all are the juncos. Perhaps because these little birds are ground-feeders and so very vulnerable to predators, juncos are "helicopter parents," continuously tending and feeding their fledglings in the flower beds, on the driveway, by the forsythia, under the maple tree, on the deck, and so on. It is all Happy Families, except . . .

Alas, we have an unhappy family of juncos—unhappy in a very particular way. This family has a cuckoo in the nest. Not a real cuckoo (like the European cuckoo) because, although there are three cuckoo species in North America (including the black-billed and yellow-billed, which are summer visitors in our region), these cuckoos are not nest parasites. Our unhappy junco family was parasitized by a brown-headed cowbird. The cowbird is related to American blackbirds (which, remember, aren't thrushes) and grackles, all in the New World family Icteridae. These cowbirds are notorious. It is said that they were originally found only on the Great Plains, where they followed the bison herds, but that the tree felling and cattle grazing over the last few centuries enabled them to spread. Certainly, now they are coast-to-coast. The cowbird produces eggs like a chicken—the female lays eggs continuously, up to seventy a year. And the cowbird parasitizes anything from a sparrowhawk to a hummingbird. Apparently, there's a high failure rate, but the cowbird is still über-successful because she can deposit so many eggs.

The cowbird starts its game like the European cuckoo. The female of both species monitors the foster parents for a few hours and then nips into the briefly untended nest of eggs and, within seconds, flicks out one host egg and deposits her egg. She leaves it to her fast-hatching offspring to do the rest. In some ways, the baby cuckoo in Britain is more vicious. It cozies up to each of the remaining eggs of the foster parents, then arches its back with its special egg-sized hollow and, one by one, catapults the other eggs overboard. The US cowbird just outgrows and outbegs its foster siblings, some (or all) of which die in the nest.

But we saw none of those episodes in the story of our unhappy junco family. We saw only the "teenage days" of the fledglings. The fledgling cowbird weighs in at about 40 grams, double the size of the 20 gram junco foster parent, and the junco parents are besotted with their Magnificent Monster of an offspring. Of course, this splendid Super-Junco must be fed, and that is truly a full-time job. We watched the ungainly streaky brown Monster standing completely still in the shadow of one of the black-eyed Susans, while the tiny junco parent scurried around. As soon as it found an insect or spider or seed, it raced back and delivered the morsel on tiptoe to the cowbird towering above. On two occasions, we observed the cowbird fly up to the garage roof, a very un-junco place to be, but the dutiful parent followed, bearing the next snack for the much-beloved Monster. But what of the rest of the family? I won't pull any punches, for the only word is Neglect. We saw a beleaguered fledgling junco get in a muddle in the autumn clematis on the eastern fence, calling piteously, and then, to our relief, wobble its way to a weedy patch on terra firma, all without any parental supervision. This was so out of character for the juncos that we guessed this poor bird was part of the unhappy family. Even worse, the black cat has returned to patrolling our estate. On Friday it was parading about in the front with a junco in its mouth. Was that another chapter in the story of our unhappy junco family, possibly even the end of the fledgling in the autumn clematis?

The end of the story, though, is that we haven't seen the Magnificent Monster in the last two days. Presumably it has fledged safe and sound, leaving the junco parents worn to a shred by the experience. It is perhaps a good thing that the junco parents lack the brains to reflect on their amazing parenting achievement in 2020.

August 16, 2020

THE ORTHOPTERAN ORCHESTRA

If you think that silence is golden and there is bliss in solitude, then please don't come to Ithaca this month. We are in the time of the orthopteran orchestra and its 24/7 program of crazy cacophony. Two weeks ago, I wrote about the daytime jet engine blasts from the tymbals of the cicadas. At that time, the orthopteran orchestra was just getting started. Now it is in full swing, and it is precisely as the *OED* defines cacophony: "a harsh discordant mixture of sounds."

Lots of players contribute to this orchestra of the Orthoptera. There are all sorts of crickets—various field crickets, ground crickets, and tree crickets. And then there are the long-horned grasshoppers (meaning with long antennae), which are called katydids here and which also come in lots of different flavors. There are the true katydids, the false katydids, the shieldback katydids, the meadow katydids, and the conehead katydids.

Is your head beginning to ache with all this complexity? Luckily, help is at hand, in the shape of a wonderful guidebook, *The Songs of Insects* by Lang Elliott and Wil Hershberger (2007). Each species has blurb on the left-hand page, a glorious mug shot photograph on the facing right-hand page, and, most important of all, there is a CD with a recording of each species. Wil Hershberger intones that number one is "the fall field cricket *Gryllus pennsylvanicus*," followed by a bunch of chirps that sound just like the chirps from the edge of our driveway. Yes, number one is an easy one because we often see the big black insect in the vegetation and it keeps on singing when we approach it quietly. Orthopteran singing is much more energetic than cicada singing, although just as voiceless. The Orthoptera don't have cicada-like tymbals, and crickets sing with their forewings. The inner edge of one forewing has a row of pegs, making a bumpy ridge (known as the "file") that is dragged across a hardened portion (the "scraper") on the other forewing—back and forth, back and forth about once a second in the field cricket. I should rewrite that because, of course, it is only the male who sings. Although it is tough music to our ears, it must be inspiring for his lady love. The wings of the female lack the file and scraper for music-making. Instead, she has a humungous ovipositor, as long as her abdomen. I can't imagine how she maneuvers through the vegetation. But she certainly needs her ovipositor a bit later to deposit her eggs deep into the ground. The eggs will sit out the cold winter underground until next summer, when it all starts again.

Two other big players in our backyard are number sixteen, the four-spotted tree cricket, *Oecanthus quadripunctatus*, and number seventeen, Davis's tree cricket, *Oecanthus exclamationis* (isn't that just a great name!). Both are slender green insects with transparent wings, and they are the endless trillers. The four-spotted just goes on and on, day and night, and tends to be low down in our black-eyed Susan or marjoram, while Davis's likes to be high up in trees—we hear it best from the bedroom window overlooking the maple tree. Well, that is what we think they are. Species identification isn't child's play. Formal identification is based on the pattern of black spots on the basal segment of the antenna (honest, that's not a joke). Davis's has two spots and four-spotted has, wait for it, four spots, but so does the fast-calling tree cricket, which I suspect we also have.

Most members of the all-male orthopteran orchestra are in tune-up mode, each individual doing his own thing, although constrained to a particular sequence of notes by the need to attract the right female. After all, the four-spotted doesn't want to be messing with a fast-caller or vice versa. But some species sing in synchrony. The common true katydid does its harsh ch-ch . . . ch-ch-ch . . . ch-ch-ch (katy. . . katydid . . . katydid), and when the males get together in sync, it can be deafening. Land and Wil tell us that the early Pilgrims were terrified by the racket (Elliott and Hershberger 2007). I am not surprised. Nothing in England could possibly prepare them for this. We are also starting to hear the first of the snowy tree crickets, my favorite, and before long there will be the synchronized chirping of many snowys from late afternoon into the night.

So, we start the summer with that sudden rush of birdsong and it is beautiful (see May 17). We close the summer with the cicadas, which will be done by the end of the month, and the mad cacophony of orthopterans, which will continue till the first frosts. So many composers have flocked to write about birds, from Handel's *Cuckoo and Nightingale* to Vaughan Williams's *Lark Ascending*, Respighi's *Birds,* and the full six *livres* of Messiaen's *Catalogue d'Oiseaux* . . . I could go on. The issue is not that insects fail to inspire. Think of Rimsky-Korsakov's *Flight of the Bumblebee* or Grieg's *The Butterfly* for the piano. But only one orthopteran piece comes to mind: "Grillon" (a cricket on the hearth), number six in Enescu's *Impressions of Childhood,* lasting just twenty-three seconds. Am I missing something, or is it that the endless confusion of the real thing is simply too unmusical? Even Arnold Schoenberg with his self-declared unlovely compositions appears not to have tried to capture the orthopteran orchestra.

George Bernard Shaw declared that hell is full of musical amateurs. If he is right, you will find me there, laughing endlessly and in pure delight at the antics of The Pianists of Saint- Saëns's *Carnival of the Animals*, perhaps accompanied by some snowy tree crickets. But for the here and now, there is no escaping that the unlovely orthopteran orchestra makes the glorious August in Ithaca even more heavenly.

August 23, 2020

BACKYARD MUNCHERS

Yesterday morning, as we surveyed the backyard scene during breakfast on the deck, we spotted a very mature caterpillar of the black swallowtail butterfly on one of the wild carrot plants under the maple tree. A good two inches long with unmistakable green and black stripes, it was facing into a half-eaten flower head, but appeared to have finished its breakfast. And then we noticed the local devastation. Wild carrot is such a pretty plant with delicate, dissected leaves and lacy white flower heads, but the galumphing caterpillar had munched its way through all the leaves and many of the flowers. And nearby was another even more devastated plant, reduced to a green stem skeleton and barely recognizable as wild carrot. Yes, our caterpillar had taken its toll, and we are confident that this single caterpillar was the sole culprit because black swallowtails lay their eggs singly, not in a clutch. None of the other nearby plants, including the luxuriant vegetative growth of lily of the valley and wild strawberry, had been touched by our ravenous caterpillar. The reason is very simple: the caterpillar has a tiny brain and anything that doesn't smell and taste like carrot is not recognized as food. A juicy strawberry leaf is as tempting as a stone for a black swallowtail caterpillar.

By lunchtime the caterpillar had disappeared, and there was no sign of it later in the day or this morning. Perhaps it became a juicy snack for a bird but more likely, it was ready to pupate. As we were busy doing other things yesterday morning, our caterpillar might have crawled down the stem to find a safe place, perhaps on one of the nearby struts of the deck, attached itself with a skein of silk, and started the complex process of dissolving its internal larval organs and building a butterfly. But there's no great hurry because any pupa developing now will need to hunker down through the long winter before emerging next spring.

Finding a black swallowtail caterpillar made us check for other swallowtail caterpillars. So far, all our other wild carrot patches look intact. We are also monitoring the spicebush for spicebush swallowtail caterpillars, especially after seeing that female spice-bush butterfly cruising around our spicebush a few weeks ago (see July 26). Hmmm, there are some spicebush leaves that are half-eaten or have holes, but that could be caused by all sorts of different insects. We are particularly looking out for rolled leaves because each caterpillar of the spicebush butterfly rolls up a leaf with silk to create a one-person tent, where it stays by day, and then comes out to munch by night. So far, nothing obvious, but we are on the lookout!

But there is plenty of other munching going on in our back-yard. One that has particularly caught our attention derives ulti-mately from our composter. Our compost is made from waste veg and fruit peelings from the kitchen, and some cucurbit seeds have survived the composting experience. Yes, we have squash and cucumber plants growing in random places, giving ground cover and some bright yellow flowers—the deer don't seem to like them. But the flowers of one squash plant last just a day. By the next morning, there is only a trail of slime and the remnants of the green calyx. I think that the nighttime slugs are finding the flowers a great delicacy—they are completely uninterested in the tough, hairy leaves. The flowers of the nearby cucumber plant have been completely unmolested by the slugs (so far) but are much loved by ants. When the flower opens in the morning, there is an ant trail up the stem and into the flower head, where a dozen or more ants are congregated around the nectaries. Well, that is slurping up the sugary nectar more than munching.

Some of our munchers are very small. Consider the pilewort. Yes, a very ugly name for an inescapably ugly plant named for its reputation to soothe a specific medical predicament. The pilewort is a native weed, a bit like a large and fleshy groundsel, about four feet high. It comes up in profusion on any bare ground in the late summer (another reason to welcome the excellent ground cover from our composter cucurbits). Pilewort sports many ungainly bright-green leaves, incongruously tiny groundsely flowers and, before long, clouds of downy seed heads that waft around the yard, setting us up for next year's pileworts—heavy sigh! Although heartily disliked by me, the pilewort is much loved by a leaf miner. Many of its leaves are marked by curving pale lines, appropriately called serpentine mines because they are sort of snakelike and because the inside of the leaf is truly mined out. This culprit is almost certainly the caterpillar of a very small moth. It lives inside the leaf and eats its way in a random walk, its jaws firmly in place at the front of its head. Just before it pupates, it bites a hole to the leaf surface, creating an escape route in advance because the moth has no jaws. Working out the taxonomy of tiny moths (the so-called microlepidoptera) is way above my pay scale, but there are lots of tiny moths around, and perhaps I should be glad that something likes pilewort.

Some of the biggest munchers this month are, of course, the crickets and friends. They like foliage of all sorts, but they are also happy to take a mouthful out of fruit, crunch the odd seed, and even feast on other insects when they get a chance. It is good form for the males to sing from the edge of a large hole munched out of a leaf because that can improve the acoustics. At the moment, some of the most abundant munchers—and singers—are the Allard's ground crickets, which scurry around on our dried-out lawn. You have to take care where you step. And that is exactly what the robins were doing yesterday evening. We were delighted to see a family of robins working the lawn—yes, at least one nest survived the many blue jay attacks (see July 19). Both parents and a couple of offspring were enjoying an evening meal that we suspect was mostly crunchy Allard's ground cricket. Certainly, the ground is too hard for worm hunting. One of the robin youngsters deviated off onto the driveway. The local chipmunk who was busy foraging for its supper there took great offense and rushed kamikaze-style at the innocent robin, who raced back to a parent on the lawn. This exchange happened a second time, after which the young robin remained firmly on the lawn, possibly with a newly acquired phobia for chipmunks.

But I will finish by returning to the swallowtail butterflies. I have kept the best till last, although this isn't about munching at all. Over the last week or so, we have had several sightings of a giant swallowtail, the largest swallowtail in the US. It is a spectacular butterfly, with glorious black-and-yellow wings, a full six inches across. It flaps its great wings as it flies purposefully across the backyard. I don't think we have any suitable plants for the caterpillar (the food plants of the giant swallowtail caterpillar are all citrus). But aren't we amazingly privileged to host four swallowtail butterfly species in our backyard—the black, the spicebush, the eastern tiger, and now the giant swallowtail. Isn't that just brilliant!

August 30, 2020

WASPS GALORE

It was in early August 2008 when I first arrived in Ithaca. I predicted that, within a week, a gaggle of teenage boys with a bucket of grimy water and a dirty sponge would be knocking on the front door, telling me that they'd already cleaned my windows and I owed them $10. I anticipated that they'd also warn me against "the other lot" who would charge more and don't clean windows properly. After no appearance in the first week, I guessed that the lads were away at summer camp or equivalent. But they didn't appear after they returned to school. Did the parents really keep them that busy with after-school lacrosse (definitely not the preserve of girl boarding schools here), marching bands, tenpin bowling at the Bowl-O-Drome, and more?

What was going on—or rather not going on? Why is this essential ingredient of British culture absent from Ithaca? Eventually the penny dropped as I started to tangle in earnest with our windows. US windows are fiendishly complicated. Our first floor (meaning ground floor) windows have been replaced, and they are low-maintenance plastic affairs with a built-in insect screen on the outside. To get at the real window, the screen has to be lifted and unhinged, and getting it back in requires skill and patience. On the second floor (meaning first floor) and attic, we have the real

McCoy three-part windows, probably dating from when the house was built in the 1930s. The innermost layer is a straightforward sash window that, in principle, can be raised or lowered to whatever height you want. Then there is the insect screen. If you have long arms and are super-flexible, you can raise the screen to any of several fixed positions on separate vertical tracks (keep the screen down all summer!). And outermost is the storm window, made of scarily thin glass. When lowered, the storm window keeps the rain and snow out and might keep us a little bit warmer in the winter. The storm window is on separate aluminum tracks from the insect screen and, provided the insect screen is up and doesn't slip, it can be repositioned by any professional contortionist at the top of their game.

Returning to the youth of Ithaca, who on earth would want to do circus tricks on a ladder with windows like this? Remember that every house will have windows of different design, each offering unique methods to dismantle and reinstall. The website for our local DIY store proudly offers thirty-eight different storm window products, some with an all-new 2020 design. After ten years of increasingly dirty windows, I gave in and got our windows cleaned by professionals. They did a great job but it took a very full day and cost a bomb.

Well, that was a digression and a half. And the only important part of that is the storm window tracks. They are a wonderful resource in the summer—for wasps.

Wasps living in our window frames? You bet! But not the wasps that come to your mind, and—yes—we have those too. Every lunch on the deck is accompanied by three or four decidedly waspish wasps. They are called yellow jackets here and, until about a decade ago, they were *Vespula vulgaris*, the same as the common wasp in the UK. But now, thanks to some enthusiastic wasp taxonomists, the North American common wasp (oops, yellow jacket) has been transformed into a different species, *Vespula alascensis*. We may also have the eastern yellow jacket, *Vespula maculifrons*, on our deck. *Maculifrons* is a little smaller and (as the Latin name tells us) has spots on its face, but we have not inspected our wasps sufficiently closely to find out. Instead, we just flail our arms around and swear at them every lunchtime. About four to six weeks ago, our wasp companions were mostly interested in nibbling out the roughened edge of our wooden deck table for nest material. That was OK until they started to build a nest on the side of the house. Jeremy swept the nest foundations away with a broom and, luckily, they decided to set up home somewhere else. But those days are long gone, and now our wasps care only about the smell of apple or orange or tomato.

Well, that was my second digression. Now I will get to the point, which is the tracks of our upstairs storm windows. Sure, these complicated structures give us the opportunity to practice our skills as contortion artistes, but they also provide the perfect nesting site for the grass-carrying wasp *Isodontia mexicana*. The all-black wasp with a wafer-thin waist stuffs the track with grass stems that rapidly turn into miniature mounds of hay. We have watched her flying to the window, with long bits of plant material streaming behind her, and then busying herself with getting it all in good order.

And now for the horror story. Our *Isodontia* wasp has created some bedding for her offspring, but what are they to eat? That requires a trip to a different aisle of the supermarket. She goes into the trees and looks for a nice juicy tree cricket. She specializes in *Oecanthus* species, the four-spotteds, Davis's, and snowys of the orthopteran orchestra (see August 16). She stings her victim with venom, leaving the cricket alive but completely paralyzed. She flies to the nest clutching the creature to her belly and inserts it into the storm window track. Before long, she will have a full larder of crickets, organized very neatly and tidily in a row. There is just one more thing to do. She lays an egg on each still-living cricket, and her work is done. Each egg hatches into a grub, which slowly consumes its allotted cricket and then crawls into the bed of hay, where it spins a papery cocoon around itself, to stay safe through the winter. Next summer, the adult wasps will emerge and fly away. Luckily, our storm windows are so loose in their tracks that, with extra care, we can get the storm window down without disturbing our wasp guests.

The euphemistically named grass-carrying wasp is not the only player in our backyard that sees our crickets as food. Our tree crickets have to contend with various other insects, spiders, birds, and chipmunks. The orthopteran orchestra has much to worry about.

September 6, 2020

THE OFFICIAL END OF SUMMER

Tomorrow, the first Monday of September, is Labor Day, a day of all-change, marking the end of the long summer vacation for the children and, in this part of the country, the closure of various summer facilities. Fittingly, it was misty early this morning, telling us that the summer is on the way out.

The thing about summer here is that it is tangible, day after day. You just can't do the great British summer holiday of driving rain and bitterly cold winds. From early June (perhaps even earlier some years) through to the end of August (perhaps a little beyond some years), we are in summer uniform of shorts, shirts (preferably sleeveless), and sandals. Sun hat and sunglasses are the summer survival kit, not a fashion statement. Wander out at 10 p.m. to watch the fireflies or enjoy the tree crickets, ignoring the coats on the hooks by the front door. In fact, avert your eyes from the winter survival kit of the coat-like-an-eiderdown, those fleece-lined boots with thick, high-grip soles, and all that complexity of woolly hats, scarves, and waterproof thermal gloves. All of that can only belong to a different planet. In high summer, it's best to believe that these days will never end.

It is easier to mark the events of the start of summer than the end of summer. Aha, here are our first hummingbirds and chimney swifts of the year! At breakfast on the deck a couple of weeks ago, we didn't know that those chimney swifts twittering high above us would be the last of the year; and does the absence of humming-birds at the feeder over the last three days mean that the hummingbirds have abandoned us too? Only time will tell. For now, we are keeping the hummingbird feeder in place, even though it provides an endless supply of sugary snacks for the wasps. Taking down the hummingbird feeder will be a marker for the end of summer. An earlier marker is removing the Japanese beetle trap from the washing line (see July 5). I did that two weeks ago, the collection bag bulging satisfyingly with JBs that didn't end their days feasting on our plants. The last marker of summer's end will be taking down the washing line altogether.

So, how does our backyard look this Labor Day weekend? In a word, GREEN. The yard is ringed by luxuriantly leafy trees, and the back lawn is wonderfully green despite the dry summer. The serious gardener would be appalled by our lawn. We have lots of clover and dandelion plants, much enjoyed by our cottontail, who frequently comes to us for breakfast or an evening meal, and the other two dominant plants at this time of year are nimblewill and plantain. Nimblewill is a pretty native grass that grows in clumps, its deep green strap-like leaves spreading horizontally from the wiry stem. If you doubt that a real gardener would hate this plant, look it up on the Internet—it's all about battles, control, and chemical warfare. If you turn next to plantain, you will see that nimblewill is just a little local difficulty for the Internet guardians of the perfect lawn. By early September of every year, the great British greater plantain, *Plantago major*, is the dominant plant, and every year I give way to wondering if next year's lawn will be a plantain monoculture—but it never is! The British nickname for this late summer über-competitor is "rat's tails," which is very appropriate.

But the US nickname is much sadder: "White Man's Foot." Wherever the settlers went, the greater plantain followed.

Back to the green-ness of our backyard, let me mention one more greenful species. We have lots of ragweed. Ragweed is different from ragwort, although both are in the daisy (composite) family. Ragweed is a native North American plant that has made the reverse invasion to roadsides and waste ground in the UK. Its spikes of green flowers are arranged on its elegant branching stems, a bit like a candelabra. Those are the male flowers. The even smaller female flowers are lower down, nestled in where the leaves branch out from the stem. Unusually for the daisy family, the ragweed attracts no insects and it is wind-pollinated. Lots of people have ragweed hay fever at this time of year. When I went to the doctor recently for my annual checkup, the doctor looked at the notes and said brusquely, ". . . and no allergies," then looked up and added wistfully, "not even ragweed," as if I was somehow letting the side down. I came home and went straight out to admire our ragweed, confirming no ill effect.

I will finish with a butterfly. In recent days our butterfly sightings have been dominated by pierid whites, all rather dull. But as we toured the estate in the warmth of yesterday's sun, there was a silver-spotted skipper. The skipper butterflies are the least elegant of the butterflies, generally smaller with fatter bodies and rather drab wings, probably rather like the first butterflies that evolved from their moth ancestors. But the silver-spotted is special because it is big for a skipper, with a wingspan more than two inches and a brilliant silver marking on the underside of the hind wing. Perhaps it was with us because the silver-spotteds like to lay their eggs on honey locust trees, and our eastern neighbor has a splendid honey locust in front of their house. But the days are numbered for the silver-spotted that honored our backyard with yesterday's visit. Its offspring must hurry up their munching of honey locust leaves, drop to the ground, and find some leaf litter, where they will roll up a dead leaf like a tent. In this protected spot, the silver-spotted skipper will sit out the winter as a pupa.

September 13, 2020

GARDEN SILKS

Being made of protein, silk is expensive stuff. And you need a special gizmo, a spinneret, to make it. The liquid protein has to be extruded through a narrow orifice with tiny spigots and valves that control precisely its thickness and how fast it passes through the hole. Get it right and, bingo!, you have a supremely flexible thread as strong as steel. Get it wrong and your thread will fray and break, or even worse, you will have a congealed gob of protein on your hands.

The tricky bit is the spinneret. Commercial silk can come only from the bottom lip of the silk moth caterpillar. The caterpillar uses it to draw out the silk protein (which incidentally is made in its salivary glands) from which it makes the protective cocoon as it develops into a moth. The cocoon is enormous and ridiculously overladen with silk, some fifty yards of the stuff. The ridiculous has happened because people in North China domesticated the silk moth for silk production more than three thousand years ago. We still depend on the lip of the caterpillar for silk, unless you go for artificial silk, a variant of nylon that is available in Walmart. And don't bother checking out Amazon or your local craft shop for a silk spinneret. They won't have anything that would work.

All of which is a long preamble to our backyard of this week, which is full of spinnerets and of silk that glitters in the sunshine, especially after rain. Our silk doesn't come from silk moths which are so domesticated that they cannot survive naturally, but from other caterpillars and, above all, spiders.

At this time of year, many tree caterpillars get to the ground by fastening the tip of their silk to a branch and reeling it out, so that they descend oh so gracefully on a silver thread. Once on terra firma, they will find a safe spot to overwinter as a pupa. In recent days I have seen several make this perilous descent from the maple and box elder. I think they are the fall cankerworm (aka *Alsophila pometaria*), and their adults are a dull-gray moth. Of course, this isn't the only way to get from the treetops to a safe place underground. The female cicadas were busy through August laying their eggs on tree branches. The first of these should be hatching now. The tiny baby cicadas have to crawl all the way down to the ground, then burrow into the soil, latch onto a convenient bit of plant root, and drink the plant sap for three to five years before emerging to sing to us (or to lay eggs) over the few wondrous weeks of August. And yes, this year's cohort of singing cicadas are no longer with us, although the crickets are still going strong.

But most of the silk manufacture in our backyard comes from spiders. The spider spinnerets are much, much more complicated than the caterpillar ones. They are on the underside of the abdomen, with a strong emphasis on "they," usually two or three pairs of them, each making slightly different kinds of silk, which are then wound together in different combinations, some with an extra *je ne sais quoi* added to make them more sticky or more waterproof. You name it, the spider can do it by mixing and matching, adjusting its spigots and all those additives.

The funnel-web spiders are everywhere, on our bushes, in the pilewort and black-eyed Susans, by the garden wall, anywhere with some purchase. Their webs are large, flat expanses of dense silk with (as the name implies) a funnel woven in at the side. We can see the single speckled brown spider lurking in the funnel. When a fly lands or I stroke the web with a small twig, the spider rushes out from its hiding place across the top of the web and . . . say no more. When I sweep the driveway with the garden broom, the spider runs out through its escape hole at the bottom of the funnel, returning later to mend the damage I have inadvertently caused.

Several years ago, we put in a small circular patio at the back of the yard, between the black walnut and the spicebush. We have a semicircle of box plants around it, now a mature foot-high border. I adore this spot—and so do the spiders, both the funnel-web spiders and the sheet-weaving spiders. The sheet-weavers are much smaller than the funnel-web builders, and we generally see only their handiwork (oops, spinneret work), made of a strong bottom sheet, usually flat or a little curved with lots of barely visible crisscrossed threads above. A small flying insect bumps into one of these upper threads and falls to the sheet below. That sheet is no safety net. Before the fly has time to right itself, the spider races out, upside down under the sheet, drags the fly down through the sheet, and . . . say no more. A tasty meal, a quick repair of the sheet and crisscrosses, and then nothing more to do until the next meal flies in.

We have one super-splendid sheet web just outside the dining room door to the deck. It is a good two foot long and shaped like a triangle with the base along the wall of the house to a point on the deck banister, and it has been maintained for more than a week so far. We had a shower of rain just after lunch today, and that seems to have caused some web damage. We watched the proud owners come out, the male smaller than the female. Both of the spiders were working at the guy ropes and among the crisscrosses. It was all too small to see for certain, but we think they were adding in extra silk and bonding everything back together. As with all livelihoods, their next meal depends on hard work.

Another excitement of today happened as I walked out past this splendid sheet web to put the breakfast on the deck table. I heard a deep croak. Goodness! That crow has serious problems. Jeremy came rushing out—that sounds like a raven... and there it was, at the top of the Norway spruce calling vigorously, while being bothered by a bunch of decidedly cross grackles. An extraordinary first for our backyard! There are ravens in isolated places nearby, and this species is "partially migratory." But I don't think our backyard raven was migrating, because we are right at the southern limit of their range, apart from a thin finger of raven habitat along the summits of the Appalachians. Perhaps our visitor was a juvenile that had taken the wrong turning. Whatever the explanation, it was a wonderful sighting, and quickly gone.

I do know that I should be telling you what these spiders are, but I am not a spider person. Here is my best bet. The funnel spiders are also called American grass spiders, and they are in the family Agelenidae. The sheet-weaving spiders are Linyphiidae (also known as money spiders), and don't ask me more than that. I am content just to enjoy their amazing silks.

September 20, 2020

LATE SEASON FLOWERS

What strikes me most about our backyard this weekend is that our last flowers of the year come in a kaleidoscope of colors, so different from the first flowers of the spring, all in white and yellow—snowdrops, winter aconites, lesser celandines.

For starters, our *Sedum spectabile* is gloriously salmon pink. The sedum is pure indulgence, the exception to the rule that anything that demands attention will not survive in our low-maintenance Darwinian backyard. The sedum has to be treated very regularly with the bad egg spray to escape being deer snack. Another fate to avoid is being smothered, whether by lesser celandine and ground ivy as the first shoots emerge (see April 5), or by the vigorous comfrey and marjoram during the high summer. That requires lots of weeding. Alas, none of this hard work can protect it from a wet summer, which makes the sedum too weak and floppy to flower. This year I have been diligent and the weather has been benign, and our September reward is multiple masses of tiny star-like pink flowers.

The sedum attracts bees—and more. The flower heads are worked by honeybees, bumblebees, wasps (the yellow jacket variety and others), and the last of the cabbage white butterflies. Temperatures have been way below average in recent days, clear blue skies and brilliant sunshine but barely getting to 60°F (15–16°C), and the insects are active for just a few hours after midday when the sedum are in full sunlight, a warm spot in the crisp air. But there are dangers. Both a funnel-web spider and a sheet web–weaver pair have set up home in our sedum, their silken sheets stretched between the plant stems a few inches below the flower heads. The tiniest error of aeronautical decision-making and an insect is dead meat. Well, that applies to the smaller insects. A honeybee or bumblebee landing on the web-weaver sheet has a good chance of escape. We witnessed that when a honeybee got tangled in the sheet web of the web-weavers on the deck (see September 13). The honeybee struggled, with one of the spider pair close by, but it got away, leaving the spiders with a hefty repair job.

Another invited late bloomer in our backyard is the autumn clematis, which seems to thrive from one year to the next on pure neglect. It covers a portion of our east fence, a mass of dark-green leaves and small, sweet-smelling white flowers that attract small insects. Also white-flowered but uninvited is white snakeroot, which sports small heads of tiny and very pretty flowers. We have several plants in a damp and shady spot close to the spicebush. Snakeroot was a love-hate plant of the early settlers because it is well defended by a mixture of about a dozen related aromatic toxins, known collectively as tremetol. The love bit was that it was meant to cure snakebites, and the hate bit was that, when eaten by cattle, it gives them the trembles and gets into the milk—and kills milk-drinking calves and people. The tremetol problem for the dairy industry seems to have (mostly) gone away because "the solution is dilution," that is, the milk of many cows is mixed before sale. Hmm, let's just enjoy the snakeroot flowers and think no further.

Beyond the backyard, the flowering plants at this time of year are dominated by goldenrods. We have a small patch of Canadian goldenrod by the garage, and that is by design. I learned in year one that Canadian goldenrod seeds freely and, if you don't weed it out, the yard is a goldenrod monoculture. Our small goldenrod patch is much enjoyed by us and by the bees and flies. But there are dangers here too. Although the goldenrod plants appear to be unsuited to accommodate web-building, they are the perfect habitat for crab spiders. These spiders are small but their first two pairs of legs are very long . . . all the better for grabbing a tasty meal. The crab spider sits in the flower head, yellow and well camouflaged, and when a bee, fly, or butterfly comes close by, it grasps the insect, injects some venom, and within seconds, it can start a leisurely meal. Apparently, if we moved the crab spider from the goldenrod to the sedum, it would go pink within a day or so. But we won't do that because our sedum visitors have enough spidery risks without adding a crab spider to their troubles.

We have other flowers that just keeping on going, especially the black-eyed Susans. The remaining flowers of lavender and sage provide splashes of purple enjoyed by the cabbage whites and bees, and there are even a few flowers of the Deptford pink lingering under the maple tree. But the bright-red bee balm flowers are gone, along with the hummingbirds that enjoyed their nectar, and the bed under the kitchen window is now a mass of big brown seed heads that we have assuredly neglected to tidy up. The goldfinches are very partial to the bee balm seeds, and it is a pleasure to watch these twittering birds as they snack.

September 27, 2020

THE WAR OF THE SEASONS

This week of the autumnal equinox has been full of contrasts. The War of the Seasons has truly begun. Winter made its first foray last weekend and Monday. It was seriously chilly, time to fish out those winter socks from the back of the drawer and so on. There was a ground frost last Sunday night in the country, but we escaped, and our orthopteran orchestra (see August 16) is still with us. And then summer fought back. We reached temperatures close to 80°F (26–27°C) yesterday, and it is set to be higher today and tomorrow. Of course, we all know the winner of this War of the Seasons. What is at issue is how many battles are in store and how quickly winter will declare victory.

And the war has its consequences for the backyard. We started the week with summer trees in the cold, and we are ending it with the start of fall colors in summer weather. Perhaps it is courtesy of that cold snap as well as the very dry conditions that the leaves are turning so early and so fast. The black walnut, usually the first to "go," is a fifty-fifty mix of green and lemon yellow, while our maple already has a bronzed tinge, and the box elder, unkindly referred to in most tree books as a trash tree, is starting to sport those dull, blotchy brown leaves that we usually associate with mid-October. As we took shelter from the heat of the sun at the back of the yard for lunch yesterday, there was a continuous stream of yellow leaves of the black walnut descending around us; and several red maple leaves landed on the breakfast table this morning. Looking at the weather forecast, I see that tomorrow will likely be our last breakfast on the deck for the next six months, and strictly indoor lunch will probably soon follow.

But summer is going out with a fight. The late season flowers of last week keep going. Our goldenrod is largely done, and the most splendid uninvited guest of this week is the calico aster. Row upon row of daisy-like flowers on the many branches of this sprawling plant, which has come to dominate every spare patch in the backyard. The central disk of each little daisy starts pale yellow and, as the flower matures, it turns to purple. Although the calico aster has no scent, it is a magnet for insects craving their late season sugar fix. Apparently the nectar tubes of this species are much shorter than in other asters, so small insects with short tongues are as rewarded as the big guys. The many flowers are worked by everything—the honeybees and even the big bumblebees and carpenter bees visit, along with yellow jacket wasps, the tiny halictid bees with a metallic-green abdomen, the hoverflies, blowflies, and "goodness knows what" other little flies. There are calico aster flowers for them all and to spare. Daisy flowers are the name of the game at the moment. As well as the calico aster, the daisy fleabane, which has been flowering for months, just keeps on budding. In addition, we now have lots of the daisy-like flowers of the rough fleabane. (The rough fleabane flowers strictly late in the year, and its single thick stem is easily distinguished from the copiously branching daisy fleabane shoot.) There could well be other aster and fleabane species, but these groups are so variable and difficult to identify. Perhaps it is best to be like the insects and just enjoy them in their endless budding profusion.

The contrasts keep on coming. As we pass the day of perfectly equal day and night, it is hardly surprising that some species have got in a muddle. As Jeremy did what must be the last mow of the year on Friday evening, he noticed that there are a few meadow violets in flower. It was almost as if he had pressed a fast-forward button to the first days of spring (see May 3). And now we have little patches of unmown lawn with our autumn violets that, thankfully, escaped the lawnmower blades. Very differently, we have a most idiosyncratic dawn chorus. Along with the blue jays, who have something to say about everything at all times, the local chickadees start our days with their piercing fee-bee calls echoing around the backyard. Are they imagining they are back in early spring?

Finally, we are anticipating another big change to our backyard lives. The work on the house of our eastern neighbors is nearly done. Our neighbors have spent their summer away while their house was remodeled by gangs of workmen who, as I've mentioned previously, are as introverted and melodious as our blue jays (see July 19). Our neighbors are due to return next week, and the human blue jays and all their noisy equipment have been at full throttle all week. They were even at work first thing this Sunday morning, their drills and chatter echoing around in the otherwise quiet neighborhood. But the workmen don't stay late into the evenings. One day last week, Jeremy heard them chatting (loudly as always) about the importance of leaving before nightfall . . . for the strangest of reasons . . . because the house is haunted. How the haunting is manifested was not apparent, but Jeremy suspects that they are conflating my faintly audible piano playing with all the Halloween stuff that is starting to be advertised. I'd never imagined that my very amateur piano playing could be spooky.

October 4, 2020

THE BACKYARD HARVEST

We now have the full kaleidoscope of early fall colors—green, yellow, orange, and red—and the daily decision of whether it is worthwhile to sweep up the leaves from the lawn and drive today or better to wait till tomorrow when there will surely be more. Day length is shortening rapidly. Sunrise crept past 7 a.m. this week, and sunset is inching its way back to 6:30 p.m. Even if it were warm enough (and it isn't), breakfast on the deck would be a gloomy event, and we find ourselves drawing the curtains by suppertime.

Another indicator of the time of year is that Jeremy has, with a heavy sigh, dusted off his electric hedge trimmer to curb the exuberant summer growth of the privet hedge on the west border of the yard. The trimming back has revealed that our privet hedge hosted three bird nests this year. We were very aware of the cardinal nest, but we shall never know who built the others and whether they raised a family successfully. On Monday (the day after the big trim), gray squirrels spotted the nests. One after the other, and possibly on repeat visits too, the squirrels inspected the nests. I watched several, and each had the same rule of engagement. The squirrel attacked from below, climbing slowly and purposefully up the hedge and then, with a sudden jump up and over, it rugby tackled the mouth of the nest, as if to claim any eggs or nestlings as "mine, all mine." Then, obviously disappointed, it rattled the nest about a bit, and scampered off across the top of the now perfectly flat hedge. In recent days, I haven't seen any squirrel activity around the nests. I guess that they have worked out that there is nothing to harvest there.

Apart from their interest in the newly discovered bird nests, the main preoccupation of the gray squirrels has been to forage for fruits and nuts. The pickings in the backyard have been rather middling this year. The serviceberry, despite its wonderful flowers in April, has produced not a single berry. The robins and squirrels have been denied that three-day bonanza of every previous year when they stripped the tree down to the very last berry. And our black walnut has had rather few fruit. The black walnut fruit is big, about two inches across (that's bigger than a ping-pong ball), and a wonderful resource for squirrels. Somehow, a squirrel can hold this enormous nut in its jaws as it races to a suitable spot for burying. Squirrels collect the fallen nuts and are also perfectly willing to harvest them before they fall. I have seen squirrels, clasping a narrow twig high in the canopy by their hind feet, while manhandling a nut into their mouth, and then maneuvering back along the branch to the trunk, and careering down at breakneck speed to the ground.

It seems that the black walnut tree across the road has been more productive. Our squirrels dice with death crossing the road, the return journey laden with a bright-green nut. The alternative route is to chase along the overhead electricity wires that cross the road. This is very much the path less traveled by, probably because the squirrels are obviously unbalanced by their front-heavy load. On one occasion, a squirrel had safely crossed the road and had obviously identified the flower bed at the front of our house as the perfect burial site, but then suddenly veered off to climb the apple tree. It parked the enormous nut in the fork of a high branch, ran down, and went back across the road. And then we saw that another squirrel was busy with a walnut just close to the house. I guess that, in the cut-and-thrust of the squirrel world, it is best not to let the other guy know where you are burying your walnut. The nut didn't stay in the tree for long, so the squirrel must have remembered to collect it later.

Just now, you can find pumpkins and squashes in serried ranks in every grocery store and roadside stall. Until very recently, our backyard sported a single squash too. Recall the many cucurbit seeds that survived our composting and germinated during the summer, giving us those big yellow flowers (see August 23). Well, this led to the start of just one squash fruit. I had images of a celebratory acorn squash dinner later this month. But, no, one day the baby squash had disappeared. More correctly, it had been nipped off, and moved about five feet from the plant. We left it untouched, and by the next day it was gone. It must have been a squirrel, who needed some serious uninterrupted time to heave this heavy load to a suitable place for a long, satisfying meal.

Our chipmunk by the garage has also been very busy. Chipmunks are much more solitary than gray squirrels, and our single individual scampers around the drive, the adjacent flower beds, and along the horizontal struts of the fence on the west side of the backyard. Its extensive burrows are in the bank beside the garage, and it often slips in and out of the garage, under the door. That slipping under the door is a little more tricky when its cheek pouches are bulging with the goodies that it needs to survive the long winter. It collects all manner of seeds, nuts, and fruits, including our very conspicuous late crop of wild strawberries. The main crop was in the summer, mostly under the maple tree, but in the last week or so, lots of the tiny bright-red fruits have appeared on the lawn, perfect for chipmunk snacking. The strawberries didn't last long.

Despite all this decidedly autumnal activity, summer continues to fight back. The tree crickets are still with us, although perhaps not as *fortissimo* as a few weeks ago; our asters and fleabanes continue to flower; and we have seen cloudless yellow butterflies on several days in the last week. Temperatures are set to climb up to 70°F (21°C) maximum in the coming week, and we will enjoy every last scrap of warmth that comes our way.

October 11, 2020

MAKING A LIVING IN THE BACKYARD

Some time ago, I read somewhere that medieval writers never bothered to say that their towns stank because the awful smell was a given. I am not the equivalent of a medieval chronicler of the backyard, but only by the skin of my teeth. The given of the backyard summer is not smelly but ANTS, and the skin of my teeth is this opening paragraph of this week's diary. How did I fail to comment on the ubiquitous ants all summer long? Armies of ants come and go across along the driveway, over the lawn, and in the flower beds, and a few crawl through the cracks in the house to check out our kitchen cupboards and the floors. Luckily, our summer regime of firmly sealed dry food containers and the honey jar in a knotted plastic bag gives them the clear message that there are better pickings outside. We see many of the large carpenter ants that nest under the bark of trees and occasionally have designs on our house and garage. There are also lots of pavement ants (probably *Tetramorium caespitum*), *Lasius* black garden ants that nest in dry patches of the lawn—and probably a host of other species that I can't identify. The robins occasionally go anting on a warm day. The bird lies on its belly on top of the *Lasius* colony, wings outstretched, head up, and beak wide open. The bird appears to be in agony. Apparently the ants go crazy, stinging furiously, and that kills the bird's parasites. After about ten minutes of this, the robin gets up, shakes off any remaining ants, and flies off, presumably fully satisfied with the ministrations from our backyard ant spa.

What jogged my memory to give you that brief—and belated— summary of ants in our summer backyard? It was a single carpenter ant, large and elegantly glossy black, that joined our lunch in the backyard yesterday. She checked out the table for breadcrumbs and other goodies with scrupulous thoroughness, then climbed carefully back down the table leg to the ground and was gone. Our ant companion fitted with the extraordinary weather, which reached 84°F (29°C) yesterday, close to the day's record for Ithaca, 86°F in 1949. To give you context, the lowest recorded temperature for October 10 is 23°F (minus 5°C) in 1980.

It has been warm enough to have lunch outside on three days in the last week—Tuesday, Friday, and Saturday. Apart from yesterday's carpenter ant, our most conspicuous lunchtime companions are the wasps and the tree crickets. The wasps aren't so very interested in our lunch these days (contrast August 30). They are totally hooked on the nectar of the calico asters, which are still in flower. It is an astonishing sight, the profusion of little daisy flowers being worked by hordes of yellow jacket wasps and the occasional bumblebee—the honeybees seem to have given up on us over the last week. It is all very peaceful in the autumnal sunshine. But as with so much in backyard life, a live-and-let-die story lurks below the surface. We have now seen two of the many foraging wasps with a conspicuous lump on their abdomen. The lump is a truly weird parasitic insect called a stylops. The adult males have wings and antennae, all the better to find the females in their five-to-six-hour adult life. The females are legless and wingless "worms" that live inside the wasp. The only contact that the female has with the outside world is that lump-like structure which accepts the sperm from the male during mating and, later, releases her newborn off-spring to the surface of the wasp. Each offspring clings to the wasp surface until safely in the nest and then drops off and walks over to a nice, juicy wasp larva . . . and so it goes on.

The stylops are so strange that they are usually treated as a separate insect order, the Strepsiptera. This means that they are as different from all other insects as beetles are from butterflies, and flies from fleas. But recent molecular data suggest that stylops might be weird beetles. It isn't clear how they are related to other beetles, and working that out will probably keep the strepsipteran experts happily occupied for some time to come. For the record, there are about six hundred known species of Strepsiptera, and different species attack all sorts of other insects. It is only in a horror movie (to my knowledge, yet to be produced) that a human would be stylopized.

And that brings me to the big question why our ants and yellow jacket wasps are so busy foraging as far into the autumn as is possible. Unlike the squirrels and chipmunks that I wrote about last week, they are not setting up a larder to tide them over during the winter. Through the summer, they had foraged to feed the offspring produced by their queen. By this time of year, the priority has shifted to putting on as much fat as possible, to survive the winter. You could say it is an internal larder, the insect fat body.

And how goes it for our fiddling grasshoppers and crickets? Well, the orthopteran orchestra gets ever fainter as each day goes by. I haven't heard the regular chirp of a *Gryllus* ground cricket for several days now, but our four-spotted and snowy tree crickets are still with us, stridulating their presence to any remaining females. It is all very much a last hurrah of the males because the females must surely be mostly interested in getting their eggs into a safe spot to overwinter. The ground crickets deposit their eggs underground, courtesy of their crazy-long ovipositor (see August 16), but the female tree crickets are not so well endowed, ovipositor-wise. Instead, they put their eggs into the stems of woody plants. I guess that our forsythia and privet are just perfect for them.

As I attend to these goings-on in the backyard, I am reminded of Aesop's fable "The Ant and the Grasshopper": how the diligent ant was busy foraging, so that it had a wintertime larder, while the grasshopper just made music all summer long. Alas, the fable isn't strictly accurate. Our ants forage whenever it's warm enough in the fall for a bulging fat body to survive the winter. That way, they are all set to make more ants next year. Our fiddling crickets are not just playing. They are setting up for more crickets next year, but in a different way. All the adults will die, not of hunger (there is still plenty to eat) but of cold, having set up the next generation is in good order. Next spring, crickets will emerge from the eggs, and the music-making adults will be back in August.

All Aesop's fables have a moral. I don't care for the original moral of "The Ant and the Grasshopper" that "there is a time to work and a time to play." The real moral is that in our backyard there are many ways to make a living, and let's not be judgmental about it. Ants, wasps, tree crickets, and even stylops are welcome here.

My PS for this week is that we've had no more sightings of the cloudless yellow butterflies since last weekend, but a duskywing skipper was basking in the sunshine under the maple tree on Friday. Jeremy identified it as a Horace's duskywing, a first for the backyard.

October 18, 2020

THE WINTER BIRDSEED FEEDER
IS BACK IN BUSINESS

At last, we have accepted the hard but obvious fact that our hummingbirds have abandoned us. Our ruby-throats, each weighing about the same as two sugar cubes, have flown to Florida and Mexico for the winter, powered by our hummingbird feeder and the nectar of our bee balm flowers. They left several weeks ago, but it was only last Sunday that we admitted defeat and took down the feeder. This was another marker of the end of summer.

But we immediately put the nail in the branch of the maple tree to good use. We replaced the hummingbird feeder with our winter birdseed feeder. This venerable contraption has a central cylinder loaded with birdseed from the top and with six holes and perches along its length for feeding birds. The cylinder is enclosed within a wire cage that protects the food from the dreaded gray squirrels (se March 22). As Jeremy put it up, we muttered solemnly about it taking some days, perhaps a really cold snap, for us to see any activity at the feeder. Like heck!

Our first visitor was just as you'd expect. Yes, the biggest gray squirrel in our neighborhood spotted something new in his patch. I write "he" advisedly as there was no escaping this testosterone-filled hunk of a squirrel with his glossy gray back, perfectly white belly, fetching black chin, and a humungous bouffant tail with silver trim, all groomed to perfection. Our alpha male was very methodical. He started with the lid at the top, but however hard he nosed it and chewed at it, the lid didn't budge (thanks to Jeremy's smart wiring). Then he dangled down by his hind feet, but every hole to access the seeds was just too far away and he couldn't fit his shoulders through the gaps of the cage. Tactic number three was to hug the feeder tightly and rock it back and forth, but the feeder remained firmly fixed to the nail (good work, Jeremy!), and he couldn't get enough momentum up for the seed to spill out of the holes. The last approach was the bottom of the feeder. This required great acrobatic skill, but that perfect set of alpha male squirrel teeth made no impression on the metal base. Clearly, this problem was not going to be solved immediately, so our squirrel returned to the branch, eyed the feeder once more, and flicked his splendid tail up and down. He was presumably marking this spot as Private Property with a drop of super-smelly urine. He then proceeded to repeat this tail flicking all along the branch back to the trunk and around the trunk. After all, he couldn't have the hoi polloi of the squirrel world eating up the seed while he was elsewhere.

Our next visitor was a surprise. It was a goldfinch—I mean an American goldfinch. It is a similar size to the European goldfinch but has very different plumage. In the summer, the male is canary yellow with a black topknot and lots of black on the wings, and the female has a pretty yellowish breast. In winter they join the club of "little brown jobs," distinguished from other LBJs only by their total lack of markings on their beige head, back, or breast. (In their defense, they do have a couple of fetching wing bars.) Anyway, soon after the squirrel departed, a single goldfinch arrived. It looked like a juvenile, rather washed out, almost pearly on the breast, and it behaved very juvenile. It was the teenager on its first visit to an All-You-Can-Eat Buffet. The little bird gorged at one hole, seed fragments flying through the air as it rushed to consume as much as possible as rapidly as possible. It then sampled from other holes in the cylinder, slowly reducing its feeding rate as its belly filled. It hopped to the outer wire, then looked back as if to check that its newly discovered cornucopia hadn't disappeared, and returned for a final snack.

After that, the usual birdy suspects started to arrive. We didn't have a repeat visit from the adolescent goldfinch. Perhaps it was traveling and will remember this Paradise Pit Stop forevermore, or perhaps it had a tummy ache from hell and will avoid all bird feeders forevermore. An uglier possibility is that our eastern neighbors, newly returned to their remodeled house, have two cats. Was our goldfinch, weighed down by all that feasting, able to keep up its guard?

This week's Bird Feeder Saga goes on and on. On Wednesday, the feeder was discovered by the chipmunk. As I've mentioned previously, our chipmunk this year has a head for heights (see May 24). It plays in the black walnut and dances on the garage roof. So, perhaps it was inevitable that it would find our feeder on the maple tree within a few days. With great energy and no decorum, it sets about filling its cheek pouches with the contents of our feeder. Every now and again it takes a break from its labor, and we can see that its cheeks are bulging, surely full to capacity. But no, it returns to yet more scrabbling of seeds from the feeder into its pouches. Our chipmunk has visited each day since then, always in the middle of the day. We wonder if it is spending its mornings clearing out a bit more burrow for the day's cache of winter food. That would mean a morning of cheek-stretching because as chipmunks excavate their burrows, they use their cheek pouches to transfer the soil to the surface.

On Friday, our midday chipmunk activity was disturbed by a squirrel. It wasn't the alpha male but a smaller and altogether scrawnier individual with a chunk of fur conspicuously missing from its rather thin tail. Clearly, the Private Property notices set up by the alpha male had worn off or were being ignored. As the squirrel leaned over from the top, the chipmunk jumped neatly from the bottom of the feeder to the trunk of the tree. It may have been a lowly squirrel, but it was a darned sight bigger than the chipmunk. The chipmunk waited patiently in the fork of the tree, its face distorted as if it had the mumps, while the squirrel failed to access the food. This squirrel was decidedly hands-on. It clutched the feeder with its teeth and hind feet while stretching its front legs toward the feeder holes. Suddenly, it spotted the chipmunk. In what looked like frustrated fury, it rushed at the chipmunk with alarming speed. The chipmunk scarpered even faster, despite being decidedly face-heavy.

So much for our expectation that our bird feeder would be discovered "sometime over the coming weeks." Jeremy has now filled the feeder three times since last Sunday, and my shopping list for this week included bird food. As we lugged the forty-pound sack of Ithaca Blend birdseed down to the basement, there were dark mutterings about its being high time for our chipmunk to go to sleep for the winter. Otherwise, forty pounds of birdseed will be transported from the maple tree to chipmunk HQ in the bank by the garage.

But the bird feeder antics aren't the only events of note this week. Looking up, fall colors are wonderful. Looking farther up, there is Mars, "the closest to Earth it'll be for another fifteen years." The sky has been clear on a couple of nights, enabling us to admire Mars rise in the west, while Jupiter and Saturn lie close together farther to the east. We could see two of Jupiter's moons with binos. It was very beautiful in the starlight, accompanied by the stalwarts of the orthopteran orchestra and the twirling fall of the occasional leaf.

And I just have space to say that we saw one butterfly this week— a cabbage white. Tune in next week to find out whether this was the last butterfly of 2020!

October 25, 2020

FALL COLORS

The backyard is breathtakingly beautiful. There is nothing special in that. Looking along the road or across to South Hill at the horizon, driving to the grocery store, or walking in the local forest, it is all beautiful. Consider more shades of yellow than you thought possible in the foliage of the black walnut, the redbud, the white ash, and many of the maples, then the gold of hop hornbeam, the orange of the pin oak, the deep bronze of the red oak, and, best of all, the flaming red of our maple tree. This hasn't happened all of a sudden, and it is constantly changing, but at a totally unpredictable pace. At the start of the week, the early morning sun glinting through the lemon leaves of the black walnut was our top number, but the rain on Friday night left our black walnut tree completely bare. By midweek, our maple was at its peak and it still looks great, even though half of its leaves now cover the lawn. Today, the birches are very pretty, a dappled mix of green and yellow against the white trunk. All will be different by tomorrow.

All week, my daily run up and down the drive has been on a carpet of leaves, which we will clear when they dry out—so that the bags that we put out on the fortnightly yard waste collection day are bulging but weigh next to nothing. Our equipment of a rake and broom makes us the eccentrics of the street. Our westerly neighbor hires a man with a pickup truck carrying a wheeled machine that guzzles gas noisily and sucks up leaves slowly. Our easterly neighbors have an equally noisy leaf blower, which they used for half an hour this week, starting three minutes into my thirty-minute online piano lesson . . .

But the technological superiority of our neighbors occupied little of my thoughts as I trotted through the leaves each day. I spent my time mostly wondering about why all these trees invest so much in these amazing pigments—all the carotenoids, the flavonoids, the anthocyanins. The standard story is that the plant breaks down the green chlorophyll into products that are returned to the body of the tree, and these other pigments are left behind. The idea that we are admiring the waste products of leaf metabolism is barely convincing for the washed-out autumn colors of the UK (no offense intended) and totally inadequate for the brilliance and magnificence of the fall colors round here. Getting so much expensive pigment into every leaf must be a costly business for a tree. The famous evolutionary biologist Bill Hamilton realized this. He infamously argued that brightly colored leaves are a Keep Out sign: a tree with the resources for such a colorful show also has the resources to defend itself against marauding beetles, caterpillars, aphids, and so on. That caused a mighty storm in the academic teacups but, as I ran this week, I've decided he might have had a point. And then another "but" came to mind: beware of single-cause explanations. So, here's another idea. Let's start with two facts. Fact number one is that a summer leaf is home for all sorts of microbes, which are endlessly hungry, thirsty, and small in number because the leaf keeps tight control over its nutrients and its water supplies; and fact number two is that these leaf pigments are well known to be great antimicrobials. Then let's move from summer to October, when all the nutrients in the leaf are being mobilized to be delivered back to the tree, so that a falling leaf is just a fibrous husk. And there it is: these pigments stop the resident microbes from going wild and gobbling up all the nutrients that have suddenly been let free in the leaf. All this autumnal glory is self-protection against insects and microbes.

By the time I got that far, I was thoroughly puffed out by my run.

I will let my mind wander no longer because I want to tell you about a much more concrete discovery of far greater backyard significance. Our spicebush, which has already survived at least two existential threats (April 19), is facing what might be yet another life-threatening danger. We noticed that a few of its leaves, close to the center of the bush, were changing color sooner than the rest, and that these leaves were bigger and broader—a bit like the leaves of the pawpaw tree down the road. Closer inspection revealed a single slim light-brown stem, right at the center of the bush. No further detective work was required. A pawpaw seed, presumably deposited by a robin that had been guzzling the local pawpaw fruit, has germinated and taken hold at the very center of our spicebush. We are considering what, if anything, to do about the interloper. Probably we will let nature take its course. After all, they may get along together, or perhaps the now well-established spicebush will win out. Time will tell.

The other main story of this week's backyard relates to the conspicuous consumption of our pin cherry fruit. This year the tree has done well, with masses of clusters of tiny bright-red cherries. Through most of the week, the robins have been at it. We think these robins are passing through. They are more skittish than our summer residents and, somehow, they look different from one day to the next. This makes sense because it is the time of year for robins to be on the move. Each robin snack is five or six berries gulped down whole in quick succession. As the more accessible berries have gone, the robins have had to be more inventive. Some dangle precariously on the flimsiest of twigs, and one pretended to be a flycatcher, flying up to grab a berry on the wing before returning to its secure starting position. This morning we saw our first cedar waxwings of the season. They are unmistakable for their brilliant black "mask" around the eyes, the droopy crest at the back of the head, and, most of all, their acrobatic skill on the pin cherry. They come every year, always as a small flock, and they love the pin cherry. Somehow, their arrival makes today a special day.

I have a small PS relating to a conspicuous consumption story from earlier in the month. The black walnut bonanza of early October (see October 4) is now over, with every one of these enormous nuts cached by a squirrel or eaten. Remember that a gray squirrel would occasionally "park" a nut up the crab apple tree to collect later. Well, one of the nuts got forgotten, and it was found by a red squirrel earlier this week. Of course, the little red squirrel doesn't have the jaw capacity for a nut larger than a ping-pong ball. So instead, it sat in the tree and tore away the fearsomely hard shell with its sharp teeth. The sweet kernel is a perfect size for red squirrel jaws, and our adventurous beast raced down the tree and off to a safe spot before any gray could intervene.

There is no mistaking the direction that the season is taking us. And yet, summer continues to fight back. Although the calico aster is done, a few daisy fleabane flowers are still with us, along with the remnants of the lavender and several brave herb Roberts. Crazily, a single periwinkle flower has bloomed this week. And the butterfly count? A single sighting—a cabbage white again—in the backyard on Wednesday. Surely this must be the last . . .

November 1, 2020

THE END OF THE 2020
ORTHOPTERAN ORCHESTRA

The 2020 orthopteran orchestra is done. The incessant stridula-
tions that dominated our backyard life of August, September,
and into October have been weakening day by day. On my driveway run on both Friday and Saturday, there was not a single chirp
or buzz, and through this week there has been no cricket company during the night. Yes, we are back to silent nights. Our music
may have died, but we can be confident that the next generation of
orthopteran musicians are scattered in profusion above, around,
and beneath us. They are inserted into suitably narrow and pliable
stems of bushes and trees or hunkered down underground. Every
member of the 2021 orchestra is just a single cell or a tiny embryo,
smaller than a pinprick and surrounded by a luscious gloop of protein, lipid, and antifreeze, all within a protective egg case. They will
remain so till next spring, when they come out of suspended animation and, using those reserves, will quickly develop and hatch.
Then powered by fresh spring leaves, they will grow through a full
dozen molts—in preparation for the 2021 Orthopteran Orches-
tral Series, starting next August. In our neglected backyard, the
future musicians will not be snuffed out by pesticides, pruning,
or any other antic of the busy-busy gardener. But they will have to
take their chances with the woodpeckers and other birds, and with

the underground predators, all of which will be delighted to come across this natural equivalent of a high-energy PowerBar.

Many contributors to the orthopteran orchestra are unseen because they play in the treetops or at the center of bushes. The other day we came across one of these hear-no-see species, an anglewing. The anglewings are definitely treetop guys, but our *Songs of Insects* book (Elliott and Hershberger 2007) informs us that they are attracted by house lights and can be found perching on window screens. Lo, one late afternoon there was a female lesser anglewing, *Microcentrum retinerve,* on the screen door to the deck. The anglewings are special because they look like leaves. Truly! The insect is perfectly green (the lesser has a little brown marking for greater realism), the veins of their forewings are patterned just like a leaf, and smartest of all, the forewings are angled up and over the body so that the entire insect is indistinguishable from yet another leaf in the tree. Of course, on our deck screen the camouflage was lost. By morning, she had gone, I hope back to her treetop rather than into a bird stomach.

The end of the orthopteran music is not the only sign of the onward march of winter. Our chipmunk is no longer ransacking our bird feeder. We think it has gone to sleep deep in its burrow. It must be the best-supplied chipmunk in New York State, set up for a subterranean banquet of Ithaca Blend birdseed whenever it briefly wakes up during the long winter ahead (see October 18). The yellow jacket wasps that so recently were gorging on the nectar of the calico aster and daisy fleabane in the autumnal sunshine are also done, safely huddled in their paper nests; and all the butterflies are also in overwintering mode, different species choosing different stages for suspended animation—some as eggs, others as larvae, pupae, or adults. But whatever their strategy, it is inevitable that some will help keep our birds and squirrels going through the hard months ahead. The big exception, of course, are the monarch butterflies, which have different hazards with their annual migrations between us and Mexico.

That takes me to the other topic . . . migrating birds. Like the monarchs, the summer visitors with a long journey have generally left long ago. Chimney swifts, hummingbirds, catbirds, grackles: these are all distant summer memories. Species with closer winter quarters are taking longer to move. At the beginning of the week, eight glorious turkey vultures soared over us, facing to the southeast. Perhaps they were traveling together down to Long Island and New Jersey or even farther south into their winter range. As in previous years, the vultures may come back briefly if there is some unseasonably warm weather during the winter, as if testing the northern limits of their range in our changing climate. We have also been enjoying the skeins of geese flying overhead, announcing their presence by their unmistakable call. Most of the geese are the Canada geese. At this time of year, many are long-distance travelers from Canada, and others are locals that are simply repositioning as the best pickings on our lakes and agricultural fields shift with the season.

But don't write off every goose skein as a Canada. At this time of year, it could be snow goose. My Wednesday run was magic because, really quite low, a perfect U of twelve snow geese flew northeast to southwest over my head. Our snow geese travelers have spent the summer on the tundra at latitudes of 60° and above, in the northern reaches of Hudson Bay, through to Baffin Island, Ellesmere Island, and possibly northern Greenland, and they will overwinter on the coastal strip of the Carolinas, Texas, Louisiana, and down into Mexico. On average, that's about four thousand miles. The snow geese regularly stop over hereabouts. In previous years, we have seen them in their thousands on Cayuga Lake and on marshland and agricultural fields near the northern end of the lake. I suspect that the dozen low-flying snow geese on Wednesday were birds moving a short distance during a break, as they tend to fly high when they are pushing through the miles in migratory flight. We will see and hear them again as they make the return journey next March.

It is not only the large and spectacular birds like turkey vultures and the geese that are getting organized for the winter. Our backyard has briefly hosted several species that could not be classified as "the usual suspects." This last week we were visited by a white-throated sparrow, which spent many minutes checking out the patch at the bottom of the deck for seeds and insects. We had hoped that it would stay on and perhaps enjoy the bird feeder, but not this time. More special was a hermit thrush on its journey south. This is our backyard lifetime second for a hermit thrush, the first being on May Day of this year (see May 3).

Altogether, winter is bounding in. No chance of a butterfly this last week; the clocks went back today, and an inch of snow is forecast for tonight.

November 8, 2020

FAKE NEWS!

How foolish of me to make firm predictions about the events of the first week of November 2020. I finished last Sunday's report of our backyard world with these brave words: "Altogether, winter is bounding in. No chance of a butterfly this last week; the clocks went back today, and an inch of snow is forecast for tonight." What really happened? Yes, we did have snow on Sunday night, but it was more like half an inch, and my chat about winter bounding in was complete nonsense. What really bounded in this last week was weather from Florida. By Wednesday, the top temperatures in early afternoon were in the high sixties (roughly 20°C), and we are set for this settled warm weather right through to next Tuesday. Clear blue skies with barely a cloud, bright sunshine, with 72 to 75°F (22–24°C) predicted today and the next two days. For my run on Monday, I was crunching through the remnants of the snow in coat, hat, and gloves, and from Wednesday onward I have been back to summer sleevelessness.

And next is the fake news of last Sunday. The orthopteran music hadn't died at all—well, not all of it. Midafternoon Wednesday, we heard the unmistakable chirping of crickets. Our surviving crickets seem to be entirely the snowy tree cricket, *Oecanthus fultoni*, named because they are very pale (not because they like the snow).

Why am I so sure? Well, partly because of their friendly little call, regularly paced sets of eight chirps, and partly because the chirping always starts midafternoon and goes into the night. Snowys don't make music in the morning, and they have never accompanied our lunch on the deck. I think that the other common species, the four-spotteds, Davis's, and so on which stridulate all day and night, really are done for this year. Probably the snowys have lasted longer than many species because they don't live in the treetops, which, with few or no leaves, are now very exposed. Instead, they like the bushes, especially the forsythia, the spirea, and the privet hedge, where they have some protection from the elements.

Everyone in Ithaca is luxuriating in this astonishing weather. Day after day we are bumping up against record temperatures for this time of year, and we have a good chance to beat the 1956 record of 72°F today. The minimum record for November 8 is 9°F (minus 13°C) in 1933. You can mutter grimly—and correctly—about climate warming, but don't be too hard on us as we anticipate our cumbersome winter gear of thick coats, padded gloves, and woolly boots, and all the fun of snow shoveling and ice scraping.

All that said, this weather is a bit discombobulating. Ridiculously, I saw a butterfly during my run yesterday—cabbage white again. And turkey vultures, which should be summer visitors, have been soaring overhead. Are these birds our summer residents who have returned from their winter haunts in the South? Or are they travelers from farther north who think they have reached Florida in double-quick time? Yes, summer is fighting back, even though the next couple of days will probably be its last stand.

Other aspects of our backyard life are just as expected for this time of year. Right on cue we have our annual equivalent of the rubber duck event. My real interest is our neighbor's honey locust tree, but I will start with the rubber ducks. In 1992 a cargo ship got into trouble in the mid-Pacific, and a container bearing 28,000 plastic bath toys broke open and went overboard. Over the following years, yellow ducks were recovered very widely in the Pacific and through to the Atlantic, famously including Woolacombe Beach (Devon, UK). Apparently this demonstrated to oceanographers that the world's oceans are all interconnected over timescales of years and that, yes indeed, some things get everywhere. Well, the rubber duck equivalents of our early November life are the tiny leaves of our neighbor's honey locust tree. You need to know just three things. The honey locust is a native legume (pea family) with a dozen or more small leaflets on every one of its myriad leaves; our eastern neighbor's tree is splendid, with branches arching over our driveway; and leaf fall is rapid, switching from a mass of yellow-gray foliage to bare branches in just a few days.

Of course, most of the leaflets end up on the front drive, but these leaflets are different from all the other deciduous leaves in our neighborhood. When dry, they are carried fast and far in the slightest breeze, and so they end up across the road, all over the backyard, and beyond. When they get wet, they become heavy and sticky. Removing damp locust leaves from the car window or shoes with a brush soon reaches an equilibrium of two-way transfer between brush and car/shoe. Add to this that the leaflets break up into ever smaller fragments and, before you know where you are, bits of honey locust leaflets are truly everywhere. Not just the layers on the car roof and front windscreen, but also in the car, even the back seat, which we generally don't use. Not just firmly wedged in their hundreds in the fabric of the front door mat, but in every darned room of the house. They end up in the washing, in the cupboard under the kitchen sink, under the bookcase in the study.

Most years, these struggles are compounded by the difficulties in clearing the honey locust leaflets from the ground. Because they take an age to dry, one can end up with unbelievably heavy bags of moldering honey locust leaves. But it has been so warm and dry these last few days that the leaflets have dried out very nicely. Our garage now has ten bags of dry leaves, waiting for the next week's yard waste collection.

November 15, 2020

WHAT'S ON TODAY'S MENU?

It has been a week of contrasts. As predicted, our weather from Florida persisted through Tuesday. We ended up exceeding the maximum daily temperature record for four days in a row, and that was glorious and worrying in equal measure. Then, it rained through Tuesday night into Wednesday. The fortnightly yard waste collection is usually on Wednesdays. Up and down the road, all the heavy-duty paper bags of leaves got soggy and started to sag in ever-deepening puddles. At about midday, we realized that we and most of our neighbors had forgotten it was Veterans' Day, and so the collection would be delayed by a day. Although most businesses work through Veterans' Day, the public duties of the City of Ithaca stop for the occasion. We were stuck . . . if we tried to move our ten bags of leaves back to the garage, the wet bags would tear open at the bottom under the weight of the sodden leaves. If we left them, they'd just get even wetter.

Ah, the trials of our quotidian lives! But the end of the story is happy. It stopped raining, the bags sort of dried out, and they were collected on Thursday morning without mishap. The only weird thing was that two of the bags disappeared on Wednesday night. I promise you, there were only eight on Thursday morning, and we haven't gone mad. We can only imagine that someone came round in a pickup truck during the night, took a few bags from every driveway, emptied the leaves elsewhere, and repurposed the tag on each bag. (Yard waste is collected only if it has a tag that we buy from the local grocery store.) If you think we are paranoid as well as mad, let me remind you that for several years a guy would come round in his pickup truck every week and check through the recycling for anything that he could take to the IthaCan & Bottle Return for six cents a shot.

After the rain and the rather weird event on Wednesday night, it turned cold, with a sharp frost on Thursday night. We are back to normal November weather, although I doubt that we will tick the box for the Average First Day of One Inch of Snow on November 20.

Despite all this, the season is closing in on us. As I survey the backyard this morning, I realize the menu has shrunk. For the cold-blooded creatures, including insects and worms, this is no big deal because they don't need food to stay warm. But for the birds and mammals, other than the dozy chipmunk, it is a very different story. When it gets cold, calories are everything. Apart from the All-You-Can-Eat-Bird-Feeder-Buffet, there doesn't appear to be much on offer.

All of which demonstrates that I don't think like a cottontail rabbit. Our cottontail, who visited us daily through much of the summer to enjoy the clover and dandelion on the lawn, had apparently abandoned us for some weeks. But there, in the pouring rain on Wednesday morning, was a cottontail (possibly the return of our summer visitor). It was on the driveway beside the forsythia bush and it was eating forsythia leaves with great gusto, despite being wet to the skin. Down the hatch went both yellow leaves on the ground and the few remaining green leaves on the lower stems of the bush. Perhaps this cottontail has been visiting us before dawn for many days, and it was somehow delayed by the rainy weather—or perhaps this visitation was a special event because the forsythia leaves were at the perfect stage of senescence to be a rabbit delicacy. I suspect the latter, because the forsythia is generally disregarded by our cottontail visitors. Forsythia is packed full of potent chemicals called phenylethanoid glycosides, which can do nasty things to the kidneys and the immune system. Neither we nor rabbits should mess with these compounds. We can leave that to the practitioners of Chinese medicine, who—disconcertingly— are reported to use forsythia rather extensively.

Another source of food is fungi, which emerged in some profusion in the week before our Florida weather, and are now recovering in the cool and the rain. I am no good at fungal taxonomy, but the *Geastrum* earthstars (probably *G. triplex*) are unmistakable. They come up every year under our eastern neighbor's western cedar tree. The outer wall of the fruiting body pops open like petals, exposing the bulgy, brown spore sac with a pimple at the top. (There are fancy mycological terms for petals and pimples, but let's not bother about them.) The spores are released in vast numbers from the pimple, and a lucky few will germinate, absorb nutrients from the organic debris under the western cedar tree, and spread underground as a mesh of fungal threads—making more earthstars to delight us next fall. Perhaps the earthstars are not a favorite menu item because we've never seen bits nibbled out of them. They seem to be even better defended than the forsythia.

Less well protected is our fungal "fairy line," meaning that we have a fairy ring, except that it doesn't form a circle. Our fairy line is the kind that isn't obvious during most of the year (it neither kills the grass nor supports lush growth of the grass). But at this time of year, it is evident as a hundred or more mushrooms. Goodness only knows what species it is, but it is definitely edible. Many of the mushrooms have been nibbled at, with a telltale line of slug slime nearby; some have great chunks removed, and a few have been upended by scrabbling of the earth. It would be tempting to suggest that our fungal feasters include the gray squirrels, but we have never seen the squirrels show any interest. I suspect more solitary and possibly nocturnal beasts take a bite as they pass by. We could easily miss the occasional daytime red squirrel, and we would certainly miss mushroom snacks taken during the night-time prowling of raccoon, skunk, or opossum.

November 22, 2020

IT SMELLS TO HIGH HEAVEN

O n Thursday morning, I reached for my winter coat and the reusable shopping bags in the walk-in cupboard by the front door, in preparation for my weekly predawn raid of the local grocery store. And then I smelled it, that fetid mix of thiols (including 2-butene-1-thiol and 3-methyl-1-butanethiol for the organic chemists who love stink bombs). It meant just one thing—skunk! I was alarmed and surprised in equal measure.

Let's start with the alarm. Quite soon after I arrived in Ithaca, a friend told me about the time a skunk got into his basement and, as he was chasing it out, the skunk sprayed his bare legs, leaving him stinking of skunk for a week. As a biologist, I should be curious to witness this astonishing behavior of skunks. From what people have told me, the skunk faces you, raises its voluminous tail, and stomps with its front feet, then twists round through 180°, sticks its bottom up, and discharges the foul liquid from its two marble-sized anal glands. The spray can reach ten feet or more, especially if the skunk does a handstand as it sprays. Apparently, most skunk don't go beyond the stomping, and they have to be seriously provoked to perform the twist-bottoms-up-spray routine. But rabid individuals will attack anything without warning, and rabies is endemic in skunk and raccoon populations. All of this raced through my head. I needed a plan that did not include observing a spraying skunk and then spending the next week in the shower, bathing in tomato juice or indulging in any of the other miracle cures that don't work.

My plan worked. I cautiously opened the front door (inward), checked through the winter storm door that the skunk wasn't on the doorstep. Then, very quickly, I opened the storm door (outward), unlocked the car doors remotely (yes, we now have a fancy car with remote keys), and in two steps I was on the passenger seat, clutching the shopping bags. Then I wriggled across to the driver's seat, thoroughly pleased with my acrobatics and hoping that, in the dark, no neighbor had seen my strange behavior. I felt doubly smug because I had cleared the damp snow from the car windows the previous afternoon. I'd done that not in anticipation of skunk but because damp afternoon snow has a way of turning into rock-hard ice overnight, requiring ten minutes of hard labor to remove before driving in the morning. I think I'd have abandoned my shopping trip rather than scrape ice off the car windows while imagining a skunk under the car. All I had to do was reverse slowly onto the road, confirm with relief that the drive had not acquired a squished skunk, and then focus on handling the icy patches on the steep hill taking me down to the grocery store.

Alarm over, I was left with the surprise of smelling skunk this week. It has turned much colder and we had a good inch or more of snow on Tuesday night into Wednesday morning. The local skunks will have fattened up through the late summer and fall. By now, they should be hunkered down in abandoned woodchuck burrows, under house porches, and, as a last resort, in burrows that they excavate with their sharp-clawed front legs. We occasionally see a skunk during a warm spell in the middle of the winter when they come out for a snack and some fresh air. I can only imagine that last Thursday's skunk had been disturbed from its winter lair.

Now that my panic is strictly past tense, I feel a little sad that I didn't see this week's visitor. Skunks are very ungainly creatures. Their front legs are much shorter than the back legs, and they lack the grace of mink or weasel (to which they are related, although mammalogists argue how closely). Our species is the striped skunk, well named for its jet-black coat with two white stripes along the back and into the tail and the white crown. It is very common throughout the continent, from about 60°N down to the northern part of Mexico.

Altogether, we have been having a rather smelly time just recently. Our other stinky events are plural and have invaded the house. Yes, stink bugs! Stink bugs are perfectly happy sucking the juices out of leaves during the summer, but as it gets cold, they look for dry, protected places to overwinter, usually in the company of all their friends and relatives. Cracks and crevices in the bark of tree trunks or garden fences are great, in through cracks of our wooden house is even better. These insects have scent glands on the ventral surface between the first and second legs, and the living insects smell foul—skunk thiols mixed in with burning rubber. A threatened stink bug can spray its stuff over several inches, and a squished stink bug . . . well, don't do it, okay!

At this point, I must add quickly that our stink bugs are not the brown marmorated stink bug, an Asian species that was famously discovered in Allentown, Pennsylvania, in 1998 and then spread widely, eating anything plant-y in sight. The BM stink bug is every agricultural entomologist's Nightmare Insect. Nor is it the kudzu bug, another Asian species that was introduced by accident to Georgia in 2009. The kudzu bug has spread as far west as Texas and north to Maryland, aggregating in many thousands on and in people's houses, making it every householder's Nightmare Insect.

Our local stink bug is more in the nuisance category than the stuff of stink bug nightmares. It is the box elder bug, *Boisea trivittata,* and a native. (For the pedants, I feel duty bound to add that it is in a different group, the Coreoidea, from the BMs and kudzus in the Pentatomoidea.) In the summer, we often see the nymphs, conspicuously black and red to warn anything from a blue jay to a skunk that they are not on the menu. The adults are dull brown with an ugly hunchbacked look to them. We think they drop from high branches of our neighbor's box elder onto our roof and gutter, and then work their way through little gaps into the house. We are totally hopeless about Prevention & Removal. Prevention means "remove box elder trees from your property" and going up high ladders to "seal entry points." Removal is all about "non-toxic" insecticides (tell me the next one . . .) and complicated stuff to do with vacuuming with noisy contraptions. So, what do we do? We open the windows to reduce the stink. We very gingerly trap singletons using a cup-and-paper and steer small groups in the dustpan with the gentlest of strokes with a brush. Then we shake the cup or dustpan outside. After all, it may take a day or so for them to come back in.

We have the stink bug problem every year. Some years are worse than others and, so far, this year has been fairly low on the Stink Bug Richter Scale. A possible reason is that, in early October, our eastern neighbor cut back the box elder branches that overhang our backyard. If fewer stink bugs are making it into our house, then where are they going? I haven't asked the neighbors yet if their box elder stink bug infestation has been particularly bad this year.

November 29, 2020

PETER, PETER, PUMPKIN EATER

It is the time of year for pumpkins. Pumpkin pie, pumpkin bread, pumpkin muffins, pumpkin cupcakes, all washed down with a pumpkin smoothie, pumpkin spice latte, or pumpkin mojito . . . you name it, it's pumpkin. And then there are the must-have pumpkin decorations, for Thanksgiving, which was celebrated this last Thursday. From the pumpkin perspective, it is like Halloween all over again. Luckily, our laziness in this respect is more than made up for by our eastern neighbors, who have decorated their front yard with lots of cheerful pumpkins of different colors and sizes.

None of which was relevant to us until last Wednesday, when one of the pumpkins had mysteriously rolled down the slope to our front lawn. In fact, most of the pumpkins had been repositioned and upended. Even more intriguing, there were unmistakable tooth marks around the equator of the biggest pumpkin. Our neighbor's display was, all of a sudden, turning into a mystery. But nothing more happened all day.

Thanksgiving morning dawned—to a scene of devastation. Several of the pumpkins had been smashed open and eviscerated. During the morning, a squirrel visited and started to pick out pumpkin seeds from a partially eaten fruit. Each pumpkin seed was manipulated in its mouth to remove any contaminating flesh and then either eaten or transferred elsewhere to bury. Despite the books declaring firmly that gray squirrels eat pumpkins, our squirrels definitely didn't care for the flesh of our neighbor's pumpkins. In fact, after a little while the squirrel decided that seed cleaning was more bother than it was worth, and it went off to be busy-busy doing more interesting things—such as the hourly harassment of our bird feeder, which remains, so far, squirrel-proof. We can be reasonably confident that our pumpkin eater is not an army of gray squirrels.

We are putting our money on deer, specifically on the local group of white-tailed deer that holes up in the wild area to the south of us. We are very much part of their regular perambulations. They are most evident after dark and in the very early morning before daybreak. During the daytime, we occasionally see hinds and juveniles, and on Tuesday morning an elegant buck with a splendid head of antlers ambled down the road. Now I wonder if he had been sizing up the pumpkins. Not with his eyes—the pumpkins all looked much the same as in previous weeks—but with his nose. Perhaps the pumpkins had to be at just the perfect state of ripening, and perhaps the deer are getting less fussy as other food items are dropping off the menu. We suspect that, while we were sleeping, the entire group came round on Tuesday night for an initial reconnoiter and testing, and the following night was an orgy of pumpkin feasting.

Our neighbors must surely feel thwarted by the deer. We know how that feels. Behind the garage, we have a discarded bird feeder inherited from our predecessors. It's a wonderful contraption and gave us great pleasure for years. The food is held in a metal box with a narrow trough positioned just above a horizontal wooden rod. Birds perch on the rod and feed from the trough, but squirrels are so heavy that they depress the rod, lowering a metal screen over the trough. This contraption was so much better than our current bird feeder because the cardinals could use it. The cardinals are too big to get through the mesh cage surrounding the feeder we use now, and their beaks are too stubby to feed from outside the cage.

But this is a deer story, not a cardinal story. A couple of years ago, a single deer (female of course) worked it out. She'd rear up on her hind legs and, with great delicacy, lick across the trough with her leathery tongue. She would then drop down, munch for a few seconds, and then repeat. In less than five minutes, she could consume the entire contents of the box. Unsurprisingly, this strategy wasn't perfectly efficient, and there'd be some seeds scattered on the ground. These were swiftly hoovered up by her companions, who never tried to imitate her party trick. If we were to continue with this, we would need to take out shares in Ithaca Blend Birdseed PLC, and so we abandoned the feeder. As I write, I am wondering if our Deer Genius might have moved on to better things, and we can start using the old feeder again. Time for another confab with Jeremy on the perennial topic of how to feed our winter birds.

Let me now pick up on the cardinals. They are such beautiful birds. The male is bright red with a striking black smudge around his red beak, and the female is olive green with a bit of red on the wings and tail. They stay with us all year round, the ultimate loyal companions, come rain or shine, blizzard or heat wave. Although they can't feed directly from our bird feeders, they forage avidly for seeds spilled onto the ground by messy feeders above. We are confident that our cardinals have contributed to the many discarded sunflower seed shells beneath our feeder. The cardinals are also enthusiastic about various plants that we have left to seed around the yard. Our bee balm heads are now completely denuded of seed, and the same goes for the cone flowers, while the pickings from the black-eyed Susans are getting slimmer by the day. The top items on the menu this week are the calico asters and daisy fleabanes, all of which sport a mass of silvery seed heads. Mostly the cardinals forage on the ground around these plants, but our entertainment through breakfast this morning was our brilliant red male balancing precariously on a calico aster stem that sagged and rocked under his weight, while he picked off one seed after another.

We tend to think of cardinals as rather fierce, perhaps because of they are so vociferously territorial in the early summer and because they are so brightly colored. But at this time of year, they forage entirely amicably alongside the goldfinches, juncos, and the occasional white-throated sparrow that also enjoy our wild seed bonanza.

December 6, 2020

HAWK, BEWARE!

The Big Backyard Event of the week was a visitation by a Cooper's hawk. We were washing up after lunch on Thursday when suddenly there it was in front of the kitchen window. Correction: she, because this was a big bird and the female Cooper's are bigger than the males. She was facing us, prancing around on her stout taloned legs with glorious orange-brown- and white-striped front, beady red eyes, and the vicious beak with that telltale downward hook of a flesh-eater. To a first approximation, she is a super-sized UK sparrowhawk. But don't be outrageous in your imagination: while the sparrowhawk is eleven to fourteen inches long, the Cooper's hawk is fifteen to twenty inches, and as I've already said, our visitor was right at the top end of the size range.

Then in a flash, she flew up to the eastern neighbor's fence, revealing her blue-gray back and wings and her long barred tail—just like a sparrowhawk's. She swiveled her head round, her red eye gleaming. For all the world, it looked like malice, but of course it was just checking for birds at our feeder. The chickadees and Carolina wren that had entertained our lunch and the greedy flock of house sparrows that we had grumbled about were gone, and all was silent. She ducked down into the neighbor's yard, and a few minutes later she swept back low and fast across our yard, over the privet hedge marking the boundary with our western neighbor. She was gone. It was a classic accipiter hawk display of astonishing speed and maneuverability.

The moment of the visitation that is most impressed on my mind was that red eye as she stood on the fence. The red eye told us more about our bird, that she is a mature female. The juveniles have yellow eyes. There's lots of chat in the birdy world about the reasons for the red eye color of mature accipiter hawks. Some argue that it takes a few years for the birds to mature fully, and eye color signals whether that bird is a suitable mate (a whole new meaning to "looking into her eyes"); others argue that the red eyes of the parent stimulate nestlings to peck and feed. Both could be true, of course.

The Cooper's hawk visitation put an end to our conversation about whether to reinstate the feeder for the cardinals (see November 29). Jeremy had not been enthusiastic, in case it attracted deer . . . and hawks. Hawks, plural, because we have two accipiter hawks to be concerned about. The second species is the sharp-shinned hawk, which is very similar in appearance to the Cooper's (including eye color) but smaller, in fact much the same as the UK sparrowhawk. Both the Cooper's and the sharp-shinned are renowned for hunting around bird feeders. Not surprisingly, the sharp-shinneds tend to go for the sparrows and wrens, while the Cooper's major in the robins, doves, and blue jays, but nothing is safe because a meal of the sharp-shinneds can sometimes go big, and the Cooper's go small.

One last thing about the hawks. Our guidebook describes both the sharp-shinned hawk and Cooper's hawk as "uncommon." This is strange. We see both regularly (although rarely in our backyard), and they are uncommon only in the obvious sense that all big, fierce animals at the top of the food chain are less common than, for example, juncos or mice. I wonder if the "uncommon" is a hangover from the bad days of the 1960s. In those bad days, the insecticide DDT nearly wiped out these wonderful birds by causing thinning of the eggshells, so that the eggs broke as the parent settled into the nest to incubate them.

The Cooper's hawk is not the only big bird we've been seeing in the last week. The pileated woodpecker has also been in evidence. During one breakfast, we watched a male rocking its way up one of the maples in our southern neighbor's backyard and, on a couple of days, a male has been cruising around, making its strange klukking call, during my driveway run. A pileated woodpecker occasionally visits our suet feeder. These visitations leave their mark. In a few short minutes, the percussive thrusts of the powerful beak transform the suet block into a mangled mess.

It is something of a relief that the pileated woodpecker has not, so far this winter, been tempted by our bird feeder. The reason has all to do with "supply and demand." To explain, I have to go back a few years. I gave the suet feeder to Jeremy as a Christmas present, along with a woodpecker suet block supplied by a famous national company. It was the most damp-squib present imaginable. Not a single bird came near it for week after week. We started to wonder if the suet had gone off, even though it looked okay. There was space in the feeder for a second suet block, so we went to our local store and bought a block of Sunflower Heart Suet made by a local company. Within a day, we had attracted woodpeckers, nuthatches, sparrows, and more. We had hit gold! Our birds are locavores, values shared with so many human Ithacans. Hence our yearly "supply and demand" dilemma. Sunflower Heart Suet often runs out in the local shop, but our birds have no way to be prudent in anticipation of the next really cold snap. We are happy for our suet to be consumed by the pileated woodpecker in March (see my very first letter of March 22), but please, please not in early December!

So, what happened to that first suet block rejected by the local birds all winter long? Nothing is ever truly wasted in our backyard. There is one bird species that doesn't care. It is the starling, originally brought from the UK to America by a New Yorker, Eugene Schieffelin, who, with more money than sense, supposedly wanted the US to have all the birds mentioned by Shakespeare. He released sixty starlings into Central Park one cold day in early March 1890, and the rest is history. Starlings aren't frequent visitors to our backyard, but large flocks live just over a mile away in Cornell Orchards. When we drive in that direction, we often see rows of them perched on the electricity wires by the road or wheeling around in the sky. One day in April, a small group visited us, and the "Christmas present suet block" was soon gone.

December 13, 2020

LIFE IN THE LEAFLESS TREES

As I survey our backyard this week, I notice that the mature deciduous trees are almost entirely leafless, and the few remaining leaves are brown and shriveled. When we look more closely, we find these leaves are on twigs that have broken off and got caught on a lower branch. That's a reminder that leaf fall has nothing to do with failure to hang on, but is good end-of-season physiology orchestrated by the complicated business of plant hormones. There is the occasional leaf on the young birch and hop hornbeam that we planted in recent years, and perhaps these saplings are still learning the hormonal ropes of the yearly cycle, while our viburnum bush and little dogwood give us color with some yellow and orange leaves yet to go.

I wish I could say that I was able to survey the yard from my daily run up and down the driveway. The trouble this week has been that I wasn't able to do the driveway run on three days. It had snowed over last weekend. That was no big deal, and it turned to slush on Sunday afternoon, but then it froze overnight. By Monday the driveway was a skating rink, ideally suited to break the leg of any wannabe runner, and it stayed that way through several days of day-and-night subfreezing temperatures. The road was safe, and so I did my round-the-block-and-along-a-bit routine on

Monday and Tuesday. This is definitely the less favored option. There are cars, uneven sidewalks, and dog walkers to negotiate. In addition, the driveway is flat, while any direction from the house involves hills. Note that by "flat" I mean Ithaca flat. If we were in Florida, the driveway would be considered a slope, bearing in mind that the elevation of our house above our grocery store is comparable to the highest point above sea level in the state of Florida—and we are toward the bottom of our road and two hundred feet lower than the university campus. That's a long way to say that the less favored run is a darn sight more aerobic than the driveway run. On Wednesday it was snowing with some determination, and even my less favored run was out of the question. Not because of a bit of snow, but because I wouldn't be able to see an icy patch or broken paving stone on the sidewalk under the snow. So I was reduced to least favored option, *100 No-Equipment Workouts*, acquired from Amazon for just such an eventuality. Stuck indoors, I limped breathlessly through "180° High Burn Action" and "Abs Defined," telling myself unconvincingly that this wasn't so ghastly. I noted with a heavy sigh that the next page is called "Abs of Steel" and will be my fate on the next day that I am reduced to least favored option. There will be many such days before the winter is done.

Altogether, I hope you will agree that it was time to celebrate when temperatures rose above freezing. The driveway skating rink melted and I was back to my friendly backyard laps on Thursday. I have particularly enjoyed watching our always busy red squirrel. It races through the branches of the maples in our southern neighbor's yard, checking for any invasions into its territory, then chases along the top of our fence and careers up and down the Norway spruce at the back of our yard behind the garage. It is always just one red squirrel because this is the most antisocial of creatures, totally different from the endless complexities of the social life of gray squirrels.

One of our gray squirrels has been very busy doing something other than the usual routine of arguing with its friends and relatives, burying food, and harassing the bird feeder. It has been collecting leaves. With an overflowing bunch of dead leaves between clenched teeth, it runs along the fence, up onto the garage roof, and then through the Norway spruce to a small cedar in our eastern neighbor's yard. There it is building a winter drey, lodged between two branches. The drey is a very untidy affair, with twigs protruding in all directions. The leaves are the infill, much needed for protection against wind and rain. As far as we can tell, the squirrel is selecting leaves from our maple tree and the slippery elm just beyond the southern stretch of our fence. Isn't slippery elm a lovely name! It is a native species and our small tree is assuredly an uninvited guest, wedged between two also uninvited Norway maples. The slippery elm gets its name from its inner bark, which is slimy (hence slippery) and is claimed to cure every complaint you can think of. But that isn't why our gray squirrel fancies slippery elm. It's because the slippery elm leaves are super-big and can, presumably, be woven as draft-proofing into the drey. This advantage outweighs the obvious hazard of tripping up while running with an oversized load that would be illegal if regulated.

And the best of the birds on all the balmy above-freezing runs between Thursday and Saturday has been the chickadee. The chickadee goes about in groups, and each loose flock of up to a dozen individuals maintains cohesion with a delightful trill of chickadee-dee, chickadee-dee-dee. As I trotted up and down, a small flock of chickadees would fly over my head from the box elder to the bird feeder. Each bird collected a single sunflower seed or fragment of peanut into its sharp little beak and individually retreated to one of several locations on the maple tree, in the privet hedge or forsythia bush, or back to the box elder, where it would snack in peace before returning to the feeder once or twice more. And then, with a flurry of chickadee-dees, the birds regrouped and were off, over the privet hedge or the fence. Before long, I heard the call again, and here was another little flock come for the same routine. I wonder if the groupings are very loose, meaning that individual birds spend time first with one group and then another, something similar to circulating around a cocktail party. And, as with a cocktail party, nosh doesn't come from a single tray or table. Chickadees vary their bird feeder routine with forays to the outer-most twigs of the trees, where they hang, often upside down, and forage for insect eggs. It is said that, in our area, apple orchards that support chickadee populations have much-reduced problems with insect pests, and I can well believe it.

Altogether, the chickadee is the chipmunk of the bird world. It makes us happy! And why? Well, it is a small bird, just five inches long, barely larger than the British blue tit. It majors in gray and beige except for its bright white cheeks and brilliant black cap (formally, it is called the black-capped chickadee). The chickadee never seems to get into fights, and its acrobatics and call are a delight that never tires.

December 20, 2020

NEARLY A FOOT OF SNOW

The backyard is a winter wonderland. A blanket of snow covers everything less than a foot high and muffles all sounds. It is a different world from the snow-free backyard. Whenever the clouds thin out enough to let through some wintry sunlight, everything sparkles and glistens, and it is pure magic. We are leaving the backyard unsullied by human footprints—no visits to the composter by the privet hedge or the trash can (translation: dustbin) in the garage. The only footprints so far are squirrel and bird; the snow is too deep for the deer. This keeps our snowy backyard beautiful for us, and it doesn't mess up the life under the snow. Assuredly, our *Blarina* shrew will have a subsurface runway across the drive from the wall to the bed under the kitchen window, and the deer mice and voles will have established trackways under the snow too. It is also a tiny statement about the importance of "letting be" in a month when scientists have calculated the depressing fact that "global human-made mass exceeds all living biomass." Oh yes, and if you are scratching your head about storing the dustbin in the garage, say raccoon and scratch no more.

The snowstorm on Wednesday night was a surprise. I am sure I remember correctly that the weather forecast on Tuesday evening was "more cold but no precipitation," but that changed to

Winter Weather Advisory in bright-red lettering by Wednesday morning, with eleven inches predicted for Tompkins County over the next twenty-four hours. The prediction was right. It started snowing early Wednesday afternoon and kept at it, with a few brief interludes, till mid-Thursday morning. This is surprising because we don't usually get so much snow in December. Let's do the numbers. In the last six years, we've had, on average, 12.3 days of snow deeper than one inch, but only one day (in 2014) with more than ten inches. But 2020 is unlikely to be a record-breaking December for snow. We would have to beat 48.1 inches (that's 1.2 meters) in 1969.

Some people seemed to be fussed by this week's snow. The BBC website headlines, presumably written in the dank rain of London, screamed about tens of millions of people in US snowstorm, and how a record-breaking blizzard slams the Northeast. Bill de Blasio, the mayor of New York City, bellowed that New Yorkers had to take this seriously.

Inevitably, Ithacans saw it differently. On the day of the record-breaking blizzard etc., the headline of our free online news service, the *Ithaca Voice*, was all about a mysterious monolith that has appeared, as if from nowhere, in McDaniels Park. Aha, Ithaca is now in direct competition with the mysterious monolith recently reported in Utah, and with the great advantage that the location of our monolith is known, and that it hasn't (so far) been removed. The other attractions of McDaniels Park are two picnic tables, a grill, and a bench, and the fact that it is "lightly used," although the last might now be past tense. You have to read several stories down the *Ithaca Voice* website to find a snow-related entry: that a snowplow caught fire outside Boynton Middle School. The reporter adds reassuringly that we should not be too alarmed because plowing is heavy work for the snowplow engine, and so these fires

aren't particularly rare. On reflection, the propensity for spontaneous combustion of Ithacan snowplows is not reassuring to me as a
resident or taxpayer of the city of Ithaca.

The response of our road to our so-called record-breaking blizzard was highly predictable. We all had to dig our way to the road,
and the road had to be cleared. The snowplow reached us soon
after 10 a.m. on Thursday. It created a sort of passable route down
the road, albeit with a heap of snow as a mid-road obstacle for
extra entertainment. The driver dumped the rest of the snow at the
entrance to our driveway. As every resident of Ithaca will testify,
our otherwise hardworking and much-valued snowplow drivers
are trained to dump plowfuls of snow at driveway entrances, especially "my driveway."

By late Thursday morning it had stopped snowing, and we got
out to dig a footpath from the front door to the road, including
through the snow mountain at the end. The first obstacle was to get
out because the winter storm door opens outward . . . into a pile of
snow. Phew! I squeezed out, and the rest was just hard labor with
a snow shovel. Neighbors were out with their snow shovels too,
and we were like blue jays calling back and forth about how are
you, how much fun this is, how we are all moving to Florida next
year, and so on. One of our opposite neighbors has the short straw
of a sidewalk along one side of their property, the only sidewalk at
our end of the street. Good citizens that they are, they decided to
clear their sidewalk before their driveway. Yes, sidewalk clearing is
not the responsibility of the local public authorities. Residents are
required to clear the snow from sidewalks within twenty-four hours
of snowfall or get fined, although this regulation doesn't appear to
be enforced as fiercely as car parking violations. It is important
to call it a sidewalk. Sidewalk is not synonymous with pavement,
which is where you shouldn't walk because the pavement is the

roadway. And talking about a zebra crossing or pelican crossing instead of a crosswalk is evidence of insanity, arguably sufficient reason to be sectioned.

We and our neighbors returned to the fray after lunch. Jeremy and I cleared the snow from the car and dug out a path between the car and the road. As we were doing this, the snowplow returned to clear its mid-road snow sculpture and the other side of the street. We chatted briefly with the driver, who'd been at it since 7 a.m. and was obviously weary. Thankfully, his snowplow showed no sign of imminent spontaneous combustion. I guess that us standing there inhibited him from dumping plowfuls of snow over our half-cleared driveway. But our triumph was brief. As the snowplow finished our road, we saw the driver make a nifty swerve to dump all the snow in front of the driveway of our neighbors with the sidewalk. The snowplow then sailed off to the next road, spraying salt from behind as it went. Our neighbors came out a little later, and I am sorry to report that they were wielding snow shovels for the rest of the afternoon.

I did intend to write about lots of other things today, but humans somehow took over. The events of our snowy Thursday will be repeated many times, although with small incidental variations, over the coming months. So perhaps it makes sense to spend one week describing a small part of what it is like in an Ithacan winter. As I write this, it is snowing again and steadily, but we are forecast to get less than an inch today. Over the coming few days, more snow is due and temperatures are predicted to hover around freezing. We have a good chance of another white Christmas.

December 27, 2020

MASS SPARROW ATTACK

The backyard dances to the beat of a different drummer from arbitrary human expectations. We had perfect "white Christmas" scenery on Friday, December 18, and a bucket-load of new precipitation forecast as snow for the twenty-fourth. But, as we are told repeatedly, weather is mathematically chaotic. The wing of the metaphorical butterfly flapped, and the anticipated snow turned into the better part of twenty-four hours of rain. So our white Christmas was receding patches of drippy snow, with a flood watch issued at 4:12 a.m. on December 25. We were informed that the steady rain of the previous day would continue into the morning, together with flash floods caused by the rain and melting snow. This meant our backyard became a very soggy place that, although sloping from east to west, sported large puddles in the dips and hollows of our lawn. Altogether, the weather ignored the Christmas imperative.

The animals don't know it's Christmas either. The gray squirrels were lying low during the days of snow. Although the squirrels are perfectly content to forage for their buried food in snow, we did not see this activity in our pre-Christmas snowy yard, and there was not a single mark of squirrel-scrabbled snow on the lawn. It must have been too deep for them. The only sign of squirrel activity was footprints from the point where a squirrel descends from the end of the fence to below the bird feeder, where the snow was thoroughly disturbed by a mass of squirrel scrabbles and bird prints. For the squirrels, Christmas Day was a day when winter called a brief cease-fire, meaning that the ground was neither blanketed in deep snow nor deep-frozen. This required ceaseless activity. It was like October replayed in reverse, as squirrels rushed around digging up goodies, right up to those ginormous black walnuts, and finding a secluded spot to gobble without harassment from friend or relative. They had only the one day because, by the twenty-sixth, the ground was frozen hard again.

I suppose we should be glad that our squirrels found some calories under our bird feeder. We could call it the silver lining of the Big Backyard Problem of the last week. For the last dozen years, we have had a perfectly sensible arrangement with the house sparrows that live in the forsythia hedge at the bottom of the road. They visit only in warm weather. That generally means that we don't refill the feeder during a brief period of unseasonably warm weather in the late fall (doesn't happen every year), and we take the feeder down when they reappear in the spring. But this year, the sparrows have torn up the agreement. They descended on us in hordes during the cold snowy weather of the last week. The consequences were dire. Literally a dozen sparrows tumbled over one another, pecking, chattering, consuming, and wasting our precious Sunflower Heart Suet (see December 6), while a gang of a half-dozen scuffled to access the Ithaca Blend birdseed from the seed feeder, spraying millet, peanut, and sunflower seeds all over the ground. We were not the only ones to look on in horror. The chickadees and tufted titmice twittered on the outermost twigs of the maple tree, the Carolina wren retreated to the privet hedge, and the goldfinches disappeared over the fence in confused disarray. Totally lacking in any social restraint or manners, the sparrows had turned our bird feeders into the avian equivalent of a pig trough. We have seen just one instance of a bird who fought back. The doughty female downy woodpecker who had been feeding peaceably from the suet responded to a Mass Sparrow Attack by lunging at any sparrow who came to her side of the suet. The threat of her sharp black beak drove the chattering sparrow to feed with even greater excitement than usual from the reverse side of the suet.

None of this should be happening. Are we subsidizing a sparrow population explosion in the forsythia hedge at the bottom of the road? Have the forsythia hedge owners reneged on their bird-feeding responsibilities? Without easy access to the bird feeders, will the chickadee population plummet this winter?

Repeat—none of this should be happening. The house sparrow, or as it is widely known in the US, the English sparrow, shouldn't be here. Just as with the starling, all the struggles with the house/English sparrow have to be laid at the door of the American Acclimatization Society of the nineteenth century. Many release sites for the sparrows were prepared, any possible predators were shot, and nest boxes for the sparrows were built. Breeding house sparrows was a profitable business, with large numbers of the birds sent around the country in railway boxcars provisioned with grain. Making loads of money out of house sparrows was possible because of two types of delusion. The first delusion can be encapsulated by the statement of the Cincinnati Acclimatization Society in 1872 that house sparrows were, in some mysterious way, ennobling for the populace of the city. The other delusion was that the house/English sparrow would control insect pests. Had no one looked at the shape of its beak? Had no one observed what it eats? Okay, it will take insects during the summer for its nestlings, but year in, year out, the house/English sparrow feeds on seeds, with a particular preference for cultivated grains. That's why a poor choice of birdseed will attract only house sparrows (and starlings), which eat anything.

There can be no excuse for the belief that house sparrows would control insects. House sparrows were well known as a grain-thieving pest in England and across western Europe. Most of the ways to control house sparrows were ugly, but one widespread method is worth a mention. It is the sparrow pot, developed in the Netherlands in the 1500s and rapidly taken up in England. Sparrow pots were hung on the walls of farm buildings in the hope that the sparrows would nest in the pot instead of damaging the thatched roof. Then the nestlings would be harvested to make sparrow pie, providing some good meals and assisting the farm cats' efforts to reduce the sparrow population in the farmyard. It is beyond me how US citizens could have been brainwashed into paying good money to introduce a pest species that had, for centuries, been netted, poisoned, and potted in the Old World.

Of course, the tables have been turned, and now there is much handwringing about the decline and fall of the suddenly much-beloved house sparrow. In the UK, the sparrow is red-listed as a species of high conservation concern, and the Cornell Lab of Ornithology (up the road from where we live) reports a similar decline in the US: an 84 percent reduction since 1966. At this point, the usual array of suspects are lined up—some plausible (efficient agriculture, pesticides, tidy gardening), some a bit odd (e.g., unleaded petrol), and some crazy (including mobile phones, of course).

None of this solves our problem of what to do about the sparrows trashing our bird feeders. The obvious solution was to consult Anna Comstock. In her *Handbook of Nature Study* (Comstock 2011), she rages against the English sparrow. Her solution was to fire a shotgun at the sparrow flock. Hmm: no problem to buy a shotgun from Walmart, and the English sparrow is not a protected species. But I think there might be a law against shooting in a built-up area without a permit. As of today, we make a lot of noise pretending to shoot every gang of sparrows we see. I will inform you of progress in the coming weeks.

January 3, 2021

CELEBRATING THE LAST DAY OF THE YEAR

Two very special things happened in our backyard on Thursday. The first was totally unexpected and occurred as we were eating our breakfast. The second was at the end of the day and thoroughly predictable. I'll tell you about them in reverse order.

As I've written so many times, we live on a slope. Look east and observe the rising row of house roofs and treetops. Look south to west, where the nearby houses are below us, and enjoy the view of steep forested hills, rising to 1,400 to 1,700 feet at the horizon. That's the theory. The practice is that the foliage of nearby trees blocks most of the view through the summer, and there is an eyesore in the winter. The eyesore is Ithaca College, built on South Hill at about a thousand feet elevation. Don't get me wrong. Ithaca College is a tremendous institution with a superb concert hall for music and the best swimming pool in Ithaca by far. But from our backyard perspective, it is best to avert the gaze because of two high-rise buildings, both of which fail the Alain de Botton test that anything built should be more beautiful than what was there before. But on New Year's Eve, all is forgiven. We went into the backyard at about 9 p.m. It was low cloud, no stars, and you'd have to trust me that we were just a few days after the full moon. But there on South Hill was an illuminated "20," the "2" and the "0" formed by lighted windows on the two Ithaca College towers. And when we returned to the yard just after midnight, we had moved to "21." It is fun—and a big thank-you to our colleagues at Ithaca College for making the effort every year!

But what about the morning event? We were visited by a marsupial. A Virginia opossum squeezed under the west fence, walked across the lawn—as cool as a cucumber—to the black walnut tree, dipped down under the fence, and was gone. The opossum won't win any prizes for beauty. Its body is an off-white barrel on four thin legs, it has an ungainly gait and a long nose, and it sticks its hairless tail straight out behind. Opossums are not rare, but they are mostly nocturnal, and we rarely see them. In fact, I have only once seen one from the house before. It was in the first winter here, and there was this extraordinary creature walking the tightrope along one of the electricity wires above the road. You can tell from these two sightings that opossums are equally happy in trees and on the ground. There are wonderful pictures on the Internet of them hanging from a branch by their tail (which is prehensile) or by their hind feet.

The Virginia opossum, *Didelphis virginiana*, is found all along the eastern part of North America, and we are close to its northern limit. In fact, one of the risks they face this far north is frostbite in their hairless tail and ears. But what is an opossum doing here? You might be tempted to think that it is a pet escape, like the pythons in Florida and the rose-ringed parakeets in London. And you'd be wrong. They came here on their own four feet, courtesy of the Great American Interchange, 2.7 million years ago. But really, we need to go even further back to 125 million years ago, when the marsupials evolved and spread across the landmasses. Remember that geography was a bit different then from now—and so it was perfectly sensible to spread from Asia to North America, then South America, and via Antarctica (which was pretty close to the equator then) to Australia. Then, the marsupials went extinct in Eurasia and North America. It was different in South America, which became a big island where the marsupials had a great time evolving and diversifying. And then, crunch, South and North America joined up, and the Great American Interchange was *on*. North American animals poured south, driving the mass extermination of the South American mammals . . . and the opossum poured north, ultimately to wander through our backyard on December 31, 2020.

Let's take a quick break for some terminology. Our visitor was an opossum, not a possum. Possums live in Australia, and they are very different beasts. For the record, the Australian possums are Phalangeriformes, while opossums, including the Virginia opossum, in the Americas are Didelphidae.

Getting back to our opossum, it was good to see it alive. Alas, the usual way we see an opossum is as roadkill. The opossums are great wanderers. They don't have territories and they move around mostly at night. On country roads, the consequences are inevitable. But not all opossums that look dead are dead. When threatened, the Virginia opossum lies down on the ground. Its eyes are wide open and unblinking, and its tongue turns from pink to blue and lolls out of the gaping mouth. Hardly appetizing for the local coyote, and to eliminate any doubt, the so-called dead opossum exudes a liquid that smells of decomposing meat from glands near its anus. Danger past, the opossum recovers and trots away.

Roadkill, coyotes . . . I haven't finished yet. There is a long tradition in this country of "opossum hunting." In the southern states, opossum hunting is a sport of the poor and dispossessed, done with dogs (but not guns) at night. The captured opossums would be fattened up for a couple of weeks before being served in a stew. One likes to think that opossums are spared this fate today. But I googled "opossum hunting New York" and found the New York State Department of Environmental Conservation declaring that the entire state was open for opossum hunting between October 25, 2020, and February 15, 2021, apart from Long Island, where hunting started a week later. Hunting hours are "any hour, day or night," and there are no bag limits. Life is still tough for the Virginia opossum.

January 10, 2021

WINTER SOUNDS

Once upon a time, I ran an undergraduate course on animal physiology that included a lecture on temperature relations. One of the studies that I described concerned cardinals, *Cardinalis cardinalis* (i.e., the bird cardinal, not the bishop cardinal). The birds were put into chambers at different temperatures and their energy expenditure was measured. Down to about 6°C (43°F), they needed very few calories, but at lower temperatures their cost of living skyrocketed. The take-home message was that it is expensive to be warm-blooded in a cold place. Every year, I pondered on whether to include this study because it seemed cruel to subject these birds to temperatures down to minus 20°C (minus 4°F), although no student ever complained about it. I had in my head that cardinals were subtropical birds. Before you raise your eyebrows, let me add that I gave these lectures in a different world: a hard-pressed junior faculty member in the UK, teaching with chalk at a blackboard. Don't tell me that I should have googled "cardinal"!

And now, let me report that, by the standards of that previous middle England self, our Ithacan backyard is cruel to cardinals. The cardinal is indeed a subtropical bird, living the year round in Mexico and the US southern states (Texas, Louisiana, Alabama,

Florida, and so on). But it is a hardy creature. The range of cardinals includes the entire eastern part of the US—and it is extending farther northward in recent years to Nova Scotia and central Quebec and Ontario.

We enjoy watching our pair of cardinals every day. They are beautiful birds, very visible and very vocal. As I trot up and down the frozen waste of the driveway on my daily run, the male (bright red) and the female (olive green/brown with fetching red accents to her wings and tail) pip-pip sociably to each other from the fence or the privet hedge and occasionally the male breaks into his melodious chew-eee call. It makes one want to believe that spring is round the corner, but he does this all winter long. Don't be taken in! They achieve all this at subfreezing temperatures, day and night, burning up gazillions of calories just to stay alive.

The cardinals are not the only ones to have made music in the freezing conditions in this week's backyard. The squirrels, blue jays, and chickadees all have plenty to say. And there has also been lots of Canada goose activity this week, by which I mean skeins of geese flying overhead, their companionable honking readily audible. They are flying in all directions and at any time of day. I am sure it is not long-distance migrations but the daily business of back-and-forth between different feeding sites in agricultural fields, large grassy areas on the local golf course and lakeside parks, and any body of water that hasn't yet frozen over. Just as for the cardinals, the Canada geese need those calories, big-time.

I am in awe of these birds, as I watch them from the warmth of the house, or during my thirty-minute driveway run bundled up in my coat, woolly hat, scarf, and thick mittens. The cardinals and other birds are adapted to this climate in a way that I cannot be because I have the biology of a bipedal ape that roamed the African savanna.

Another sound that we hear very frequently in the cold winter air reminds us that our region hasn't always had Narnia-like winters. It is the hooting of the freight trains on the Ithaca Central Railroad, transporting rock salt from the Cayuga Salt Mine for use on the winter roads throughout the Northeast of the country. During the Silurian Period (that's more than 400 million years ago), most of the continent was a warm shallow sea, so shallow in the Ithaca area that salt deposits often evaporated out. The Cayuga Salt Mine opens to the surface just ten miles up the road along the edge of Cayuga Lake. The mine is 2,300 feet deep, running under the lake over a very extensive area. It is big business and big local politics. The mine is owned by the international conglomerate Cargill, the antithesis of an Ithacan cooperative. Cargill is accused by some people of polluting Cayuga Lake with salt and failing to disclose information about the risks and consequences of subsidence and mine collapse for freshwater life and our drinking water. Despite the hoo-ha, I don't anticipate the hooting of the salt train to be discontinued soon.

I have one last backyard sound to write about for this week. This sound is made by humans, just like the salt train hoots, but it is musical. It is the recent concerts of Cornell bell tower chimes that have been played over the holiday season until last Tuesday, the fifth. There are twenty-one bells, some of which date back to 1868, just a few years after the university opened, and most of the chimes masters are students. The bell ringers have been playing song requests, from ABBA to Bach, Christmas carols, and much more. We are very well positioned to hear the chimes, being about a mile downhill from the Cornell bell tower. When the air has been still, we can hear them from the yard, and when a good northerly is blowing (that's fairly often), we can listen to them from inside the house.

I realize that I was a little economical with the truth when I wrote that we are downhill from the bell tower. It is not that simple. There is a stonking great gorge between us. And that gives me the excuse to turn to something that I have been meaning to write about lots of times. Why is our local world so hilly? Why are so many local bumper stickers, T-shirts, aprons, fridge magnets, and you-name-it adorned with "Ithaca Is Gorges"?

For "Ithaca Is Gorges," we need to go to a more recent past than the salt mines, and one far colder and even less hospitable than today. It is the repeated ice ages of the last two million years, with great glaciers that came and went. When they came to our region, they gouged out river valleys that drained south to north, and they scoured the gently sloping valley sides into the fearsomely steep hills that we negotiate every day. When the glaciers receded, they left behind river valleys dammed by glacial sediment, creating our long, thin, and deep Finger Lakes. One more thing before I get to the gorges. Cayuga Lake is so deep that it goes below sea level. (If you are a numbers fan, it's 435 feet deep; the bottom is fifty-three feet below sea level, with another four hundred feet of sediment before you get to rock.) Cargill is mining salt well below that! Now to the gorges. These are east-west-directed streams, the equivalent of the tributaries of the old river valleys. They career down the glacier-steepened slopes, cascading as waterfalls as they pass from seams of hard bedrock to easily erodible layers of soft bedrock. A note for the geologically minded: our bedrock is Upper Devonian sandstone, siltstone, and shale, laid down after the Silurian salts—obviously.

January 17, 2021

SPARROW WARS

We are at our wits' end! The bird feeders in the backyard are now an integral part of the daily feeding routine for the house sparrows that live in the forsythia hedge at the bottom of the road. At regular intervals through every day, a gang of sparrows descends on the feeders suspended from a lower branch of our maple tree. They gorge themselves at great speed and with no manners, spraying seeds and fragments of suet all over the place. This means that our feeder refilling rate has switched from once per two weeks to once per two days. The discarded food below is hoovered up, mostly by the squirrels, and the area of general trampling and disturbance on the ground has expanded dramatically, putting our Lenten rose and lily of the valley bulbs at risk. Why aren't the sparrows ignoring us through the winter, as in previous years?

Over the last three weeks, we have applied Anna Comstock's procedure to deter the sparrow gang. As I explained on December 27, her solution is to fire a shotgun at them. We modified her protocol to making a loud noise while pointing a stick at them. Alas, that didn't work especially well, and we quickly discovered that the Black Bear Routine is more effective than the Anna Comstock protocol. Scare them away by waving your arms around wildly while making lots of noise. In the first week or so, the sparrows responded by flying swiftly over the privet hedge, and we heard and saw no more of them for a while. But before long, they realized that our intervention wasn't dangerous and required nothing more than a tactical retreat to the privet hedge for a bit of excited chatter until we went away. By week two, we had adopted a variant of the Black Bear Routine: a quick sprint across the lawn, stick in hand to beat the privet hedge while yelling fiercely. But that only postponed the mass attack by about five minutes and had the disadvantage that our neighbors must be concluding that we were reenacting that *Fawlty Towers* episode when Basil, bellowing loudly, beats a car with a stick. Note that the last sentence is in the past tense. In the last few days, the sparrows have responded to the Basil Fawlty protocol by flying not into the privet hedge but high up in the maple tree. They chatter contentedly among themselves, looking down at me as I jump up and down, yelling and gesticulating in vain, and then return to the feeders as soon as they hear the house door click shut behind me.

Three weeks ago, our biggest concern was that our sparrow-scaring routines would scare the other birds more than the sparrows. Remarkably, this hasn't happened. When the sparrow mob descends on the feeders, they oust any other bird that might be there. The chickadees and tufted titmice fly to the outermost branches and twigs of the maple tree, the nuthatches back to the trunk, and the juncos to the bottom of our forsythia bush. While the sparrow–human conflict is played out, they can be seen foraging for natural foods. The nuthatches work their zigzag way down the trunk and tweak out a goodie with their sharp beaks, the chickadees dangle from the twigs as they forage for insect eggs, and the juncos check out the edge of the driveway for seeds. Then, once the sparrows are gone, they return for a peanut, piece of millet, or sunflower seed.

We have to applaud the sparrows—even if through gritted teeth! They outcompete other bird species by dint of numbers, and their collective behavior is remarkably flexible.

Thinking for a moment, we shouldn't really be surprised by the success of house sparrows. Anna Comstock's description of them as English sparrows is accurate only in a parochial sense, that they were brought across to the US from England. Really, house sparrows started out in the Middle East, where, with the advent of human agriculture about ten thousand years ago, they switched from being migratory birds that lived in natural grasslands to life with humans. The early farmers offered them a lifestyle makeover, with a year-round supply of food from grain stores and scraps from feeding themselves and their newly domesticated animals, as well as nest sites in their houses. And wherever the humans went, the house sparrow followed. Today, house sparrows live almost entirely in human-dominated places and they have the dubious distinction of being the most widely distributed of all bird species. They couldn't have achieved this if they weren't well attuned to human behavior. You may think your dog knows what you are thinking, but from my experience of the last three weeks, I can assure you that so does your gang of house sparrows.

Back to our backyard: the house sparrows are making us question our bird feeding. Why do we feed the birds? Well, we greatly enjoy seeing the birds at the feeders, but inescapably saving the birds is also part of our rationale. There have been so many studies on how wintertime supplementary feeding influences the populations of small birds, especially the great tits and blue tits in Europe and the chickadees in North America. In some places and years, the extra food has no effect on the bird populations; but when it is really cold, the supplementary feeding saves many individual birds. It is also obvious that the birds (other than the house sparrows) in our backyard don't eat the feeder food to the exclusion of natural foods, even though it is so easy to eat as much of the feeder food as they want. That's not so very surprising. After all, each species has its own particular dietary needs, which are unlikely to be met by the limited variety in the feeder foods. And we are scrupulously negligent gardeners, so that the birds have as much of their natural foods as the backyard can offer.

The other issue is the consequences of winter-feeding house sparrows. One thing for sure is that we are subsidizing our local house sparrow population. There will be more house sparrows competing for nesting sites next May. And these birds are vicious. They don't recognize sitting tenant rights of other species, and they happily oust other birds from a nest site, breaking any eggs and killing any nestlings. Anna Comstock knew all about this. As well as her shotgun protocol, she recommends that any sparrow nests should be destroyed, noting that this activity helps the sparrows recognize that they aren't welcome. There's no mistaking that Anna Comstock held no hostages in her Sparrow Wars. Clearly, we need to think ahead as we decide our next move in our Sparrow War.

Enough of house sparrows. I want to mention briefly a different bird gang event that happened on Friday morning. A red-tailed hawk paid a visit, not to the backyard but to a small tree of our northerly neighbor on the other side of the road. Red-tails are big hawks, larger than the Cooper's hawk that visited last year (see December 6), but with a proportionately much shorter tail—which is red. This visitation caused uproar. Two crows started it off, cawing with great gusto from a nearby electricity wire while glaring directly at the hawk. This noise attracted all the blue jays in the neighborhood, and they pranced around excitedly in our crab apple tree and in our neighbor's black walnut tree, screaming "jeer—jeer—jeer" repeatedly. Even the male cardinal got in on the act, pipping vigorously from the pin cherry. The red-tail got the hint, realizing that any element of surprise in its search for lunch had been completely destroyed. It flew off gracefully in search of a place with a less active Neighborhood Watch community.

January 24, 2021

THE DAILY RED SQUIRREL

Several years ago, we went to an opera at the Met in New York City with a friend who is an opera buff. The show was dazzling. For every scene, we were transported to a different world created by extravagant scenery of immaculately carpentered wood and exotic fabrics, together with ever-changing music from the singers and orchestra; and the enormous stage accommodated several crowd scenes of countless gloriously clad singers. It was a different world from Ithaca theater. Time and again, we have enjoyed Ithacan plays with scripts selected to match the single-digit cast (who may be called upon to double up as the benevolent grandpa and the villain's henchman), and a simple stage backdrop made of plywood, perhaps transitioning between a curtain to indicate "indoors" and a bunch of plastic flowers to signal "in the forest of Arden."

I mention this because there are some parallels to summer versus winter in our backyard. Summer is full of color and song with an endless cast of players, many of whom come and go. The winter scene changes little from one day to the next—at least in the lulls between the storms (aka the "winter weather" of the "winter weather advisory"). We open the curtains every morning to a world of mostly gray, bounded by the gaunt black walnut and maple, and comment that there may have been a bit more snow last night—or not. Compounding that sense of being stuck in the same scene, the small number of players acting out on the back-yard stage change little from one day to the next.

Let me swiftly add that the parallels between Ithaca winter and Ithaca theater break down very swiftly. We are Ithaca theater enthusiasts and we have been to the Metropolitan Opera House only the once; but we are Ithaca summer enthusiasts and our attitude to Ithaca winter is to "get on with it." I am reminded of the pep talk given by a good colleague to freshman students returning for their second semester in late January. In bracing tones he declares, "To survive the winter, you have to embrace the winter," to a circle of numb students from Florida, Texas, and California, still wearing unlined jackets and two-ply gloves. But before long, every surviving student is decked out in a padded North Face coat (or, if rich, a Canada Goose parka), and gloves that mean business, together with woolen scarf and hat.

We appreciate almost all our winter regulars in the backyard, and this week I am bringing the red squirrel into the spotlight. The center of its universe is the row of Norway spruce running from the southeast corner of our yard along the boundary between our southern and southeastern neighbors. To digress for a moment, our neighborhood has lots of mature Norway spruce, singletons or rows or clumps. Perhaps a truck laden with saplings rolled through soon after the houses were built in the 1930s. And I wonder whether it was the proud first owners who planted the trees at the boundaries of their property or if a bunch of spade-wielding people supported by Roosevelt's Civil Works Administration accompanied the truck. However it all started, these Norway spruce are now mature trees and a haven for the red squirrel. Anna Comstock comments on how the red squirrel tackles a Norway spruce cone:

first, it tears the cone apart, and then, among the many dissected scales, it forages for the tasty seeds (Comstock 1911). Very likely our red squirrel's home base is a tree hole, perhaps hollowed out by a pileated woodpecker. Although red squirrels can make a leaf nest when no prefab holes are available, we haven't spotted any sign of one in our Norway spruce or other nearby trees.

We see our red squirrel every morning at breakfast. Dawn is breaking, and there it is! Our red squirrel has an invariant loop. It goes clockwise through the maples of our east and southeast neighbors, across to our black walnut at a level just above the fence, then vertically up almost to the top, as fast as along the horizontal branches, followed by a wild leap across to the Norway spruce for a final check around all the branches of home base. It all looks like a crazy, breathless dash, as if the squirrel is driven to race its circuit faster than yesterday. The leaps from the terminal twigs of one tree to the next look reckless in the extreme, and it astonishes me that its little claws are sharp and strong enough to secure every step of the chase up the vertical trunk of the black walnut. If Hollywood had invented red squirrels, it would have given them feet with suction pads to make their acrobatics plausible.

Before we go any further, I need to remind you that the American red squirrel is not the same species as the European red squirrel. In fact, they are not closely related at all. The European red squirrel is actually a close relative of the American gray squirrel that the squirrel-brained Mr. Brocklehurst released on his Henbury Park in Cheshire on that fateful day in 1876 (see April 26). To be formal for a moment, the gray and European red are both *Sciurus*, and the American red is *Tamiasciurus*. The American reds are seriously small, weighing just six ounces. That's the same weight as three tennis balls, and a little over one-half of the weight of the European red and one-third of the weight of the gray squirrel.

We occasionally see the red squirrel during the day as it forages for nuts and seeds, as well as nibbling at the buds of the Norway spruce trees. Our squirrel rarely ventures onto the ground in our backyard, and we guess that all those pine cones, nuts, and fungi that it collected last fall must be buried elsewhere. Perhaps this year's red is more timid than the occupants of the Norway spruces in some previous years, or perhaps it is very savvy and is avoiding all the neighborhood cats that prowl around. Inescapably, the personalities of the backyard animals change from one year to the next. Our red squirrel of the 2012–13 winter was a superstar, so adventurous that it visited the bird feeder by the deck. It discovered that it was small enough to squeeze through the gray squirrel barrier, and it feasted on Ithaca Blend birdseed every day for weeks. The superstar must have moved on to other things because that was a one-winter wonder.

As I read what I have written so far, I see the need to make a correction. We may feel that we are "stuck in the same scene" of a wintry wasteland, but that is not true. Things are changing. Our day length has increased from the minimum on December 21 of nine hours, four minutes (yes, we are at a much lower latitude than the UK!), to all of nine hours, forty-nine minutes today, and although our average temperature for January is 23.3°F (that's minus 4.8°C), we will increase to a blistering average of 25.3°F (minus 3.7°C) in February. Actually, there is so much variation in the temperature that these averages are rather meaningless except in the sense that any red squirrel, however timid, has to be a superstar survivor. The day length, and particularly the time of sunrise, is much more important. Just now, the red squirrel morning show happens just after dawn at 7:26 a.m., beautifully timed to be savored over breakfast coffee. But by March 13, the day before the clocks go forward, we will have to have a 6:20 a.m. breakfast to enjoy the daily gymnastic display.

January 31, 2021

IT IS NOTHING BUT WINTER—
WINTER, COLD AND SAVAGE

The title for today's letter perfectly encapsulates the backyard this week. It is from number 18 of Schubert's song cycle *Winterreise*. We listened to a recording during the winter holiday break, when our temperatures were above freezing. It is haunting music, more forlorn than the bleakest Shostakovich, more hypnotic than the most unremitting Glass. And then, in the eighteenth song, there were these words: "It is nothing but winter—winter, cold and savage." It was as if Schubert had experienced Ithaca, New York, in late January. Fast-forward a month to the last day of January. The yard has a six-inch blanket of snow, and the temperature is "17°F, feels like 10°F" (minus 8°C/minus 12°C), and this is the second day in a row that the Ithaca weather website cheerfully describes as "*MUCH WARMER* than yesterday." At this midmorning time on Friday it was 12°F, feels like minus 2°F (minus 11°C /minus 19°C). As I started . . . the title perfectly encapsulates the backyard this week.

But, unlike Schubert (or, more correctly, the poet Wilhelm Müller), whose journey went nowhere (like Kafka or Ishiguro's *Unconsoled*), my journey today will take us through the year, including some days of high summer. That's to keep us cheerful! My starting point is the end point of every conversation at this time of year with my good colleagues in Geneva. These conversations always gravitate to whether it will be "a good season" this year. Let me explain. I am referring to colleagues based at the New York State Agricultural Experimental Station (recently rebranded Cornell AgriTech) in the small city of Geneva, New York (population around thirteen thousand), at the northern end of Lake Seneca, about fifty miles from Ithaca. My colleagues are applied entomologists with the responsibility to mitigate insect pests on crops grown by New York farmers. They spend the summer investigating whether a new spray will protect apples against the apple maggot, whether predatory mites might reduce the depredations of onion thrips, how sowing dates or crop rotation can reduce carrot root fly, and so on. But their experiments need the pests to be there in good numbers. If the winter deep freeze is particularly cold or long, then few of their pests make it to the spring. Then the farmers are happy, but the Geneva experiments are thwarted. All this is telling us that "winter, cold and savage" does much to shape how the following summer unfolds.

Apple maggots, onion thrips, and carrot root flies are not obvious players in our backyard, but they have one thing in common with some of our big summer players: that they spend the winter underground. I am thinking particularly of the next generation of Japanese beetles that eat their way through our July backyard (July 5), and the cicadas that serenade us through August breakfasts on the deck (August 2). Today, these insects are safe under our feet as we wade through the snow, taking our vegetable peelings to the composter at the far end of the lawn.

In fact, I know exactly how those pesky Japanese beetle grubs are getting on, thanks to a wonderful website on the local soil temperatures. Today it is 32°F (0°C) down to four inches, meaning that it's frozen that far down. The temperature rises gradually to 37°F (nearly 3°C) at two feet under. Japanese beetle grubs die if they freeze, and they don't make any good antifreeze, so their sole winter task is to adjust their depth as the temperatures slowly shift. Most years, this strategy works. But the website also tells me that occasionally (for example, in January 2015) the soil can freeze right down to two feet, and I suspect that would spell disaster for many Japanese beetle grubs.

The Japanese beetles spend most of their twelve-to-thirteen-month lifespan adopting a low profile as grubs in cold soil. In the heat of last July, egg-heavy females took a daily break from eating our plants at about teatime in the afternoon. Each insect climbed down the stem of the plant she'd been defoliating, scraped out a small hole in the soil, and deposited about five eggs, covered them over, and then returned to the feeding party. After the eggs hatched, the grubs stayed in the soil, eating the roots of plants, especially the grass of our lawn. They kept on eating and growing till the temperature dropped to about 50°F (10°C). From then on, they have just existed in the dark and cold with the single imperative "I must not freeze." When the soil gets warm enough (about mid-May), they will eat some more roots, complete their development to adulthood . . . and emerge for a few weeks of leaf eating, mating, and egg laying in the July sunshine. It is a winning strategy, provided it doesn't get too cold in January and February. Today's blanket of snow is good insulation. We will need plummeting temperatures with no snow to prevent the annual horde of Japanese beetle in our backyard next summer.

But if it freezes to a great depth, then our cicadas are at risk! They are safe underground and, just like the beetle grubs, they adjust their depth by temperature. The ghostly-white cicada nymphs walk up, down, and along the network of roots under our lawn on their tiny legs in the pitch black. When in a good place, these insects tap into the water vessels of the roots of our maple tree with jaws modified into fine needles. They have to pump hard for little sustenance at this time of year, but they are in no hurry. A baby cicada is pure patience, waiting for the tree sap to rise in the spring, and growing slowly through a full four to five years before a glorious three or four weeks of adult life in the warmth and sunshine of August.

Of course, not all insects overwinter in the soil. There are many hazards, from drowning in snowmelt to being on the menu of our hungry *Blarina* shrew or the next flock of starlings probing their beaks deep into the soil. If an insect can make enough antifreeze or tolerate a few ice crystals in their blood, staying above ground is a sensible strategy. Mind you, the choice could reduce to: "Would you rather be eaten by a starling or a chickadee?" Luckily for the chickadees, many insects opt for above ground.

There is one important above-ground survivor of "winter, cold and savage" that somehow slipped the net of my letters last summer. This is the goldenrod gall fly, *Eurosta solidaginis*. Today's backyard population of goldenrod gall flies are, like the Japanese beetles and cicadas, all immature, but, unlike the other two species, they could be counted precisely if we were motivated. This is because there is one maggot per gall, and the galls are very obvious. Each gall is a big ball-like swelling on the dead skeleton stem of Canada goldenrod. The maggot is perfectly still, stuffed full of antifreeze (sorbitol, to be precise), and it may even be a bit frozen. Amazingly, freezing is okay for a goldenrod gall fly maggot. And how did it get there? Well, last summer, the female fly laid her eggs just below the emerging buds of a goldenrod. The hatchling from one of those eggs chewed out a home inside the stem and persuaded the stem to make a big cavity with thick walls and luscious protein-rich tissues on the inner surface. The maggot spit must contain chemicals that imitate plant hormones. Anyway, the maggot eats and grows on this endlessly renewing plant nosh, well protected from predators, until fall. Then it chews out an exit hole, except for an outermost paper-thin layer, and settles down for the winter. When it warms up in the spring, it becomes adult. The fly then pumps blood into its head to blast its way through that final layer of the exit tunnel into summer sunshine. Some quick matings and egg laying and that's it, hand over to the next generation. The adults don't feed in their week in the sun.

Truly, life is tough! Yet again, I realize that I am just a blink of the eye from my ancestors in the African savanna. It is only because our extraordinary culture gives me warmth and food that I can enjoy the beauty of Ithaca at this time of year and admire everything in the backyard that is adapted to survive "winter, cold and savage."

February 7, 2021

A MILLER B NOR'EASTER AND
A BUMPUS EVENT

It was last Sunday morning that *Ithaca Voice*, our local news website, alerted us to expect a Miller Type B nor'easter. The article then explained that Type B, as designated by J. E. Miller in 1946, starts up as a depression inland, this time in the Ohio Valley. When this low pressure hits the Appalachians and weakens, it somehow creates a second depression to the east near the coast. That's when things start to happen fast and furious. Weather from the Atlantic seaboard of Canada is rapidly sucked in, bringing in lots of cold, wet air and snow . . . and more snow . . . and yet more snow. This week's Miller B lasted from Sunday lunchtime to Wednesday lunchtime.

Over the full three days, we watched our backyard landscape disappear. As the snow level rose, slowly but inexorably, we lost the dwarf sumac by the privet hedge, then the juniper bushes by the garage were gone, then the little box hedge next to the spicebush, and so on. Our backyard world today is simple, made up of trees emerging from a smooth counterpane of bright, glistening white. Of course, it is different and much more energetic at the front. We did snow shoveling exercise twice a day to ensure that we could get out of the front door and walk to the road, and to clear the daily snow mountain dumped in our driveway by the city snowplow (see December 20).

Our backyard life has seen it all before, and everything knows the ropes. Just as we hunkered down for the three days in our house, the birds and the squirrels hunkered down in tree holes and in the middle of large bushes. We discovered that we have created an extra snowstorm habitat for the birds. Last fall we pruned back the redbud and put the branches in the narrow gap between the garage and the eastern fence. This was as an obstacle against deer coming in from behind the garage and as a barrier against the local cats, which were getting too interested in the chipmunk burrow in the bank beside the garage. The strategy has worked with the bonus of providing a well-protected tangle of branches and twigs where our normally ground-loving juncos could sit out the storm in safety. Under the juncos and more than a foot of snow, the chipmunk is snoozing gently in its labyrinth of tunnels. Every now and again, it wakes up briefly, stretches, and nibbles on the Ithaca Blend birdseed that it purloined from our bird feeder last October (see October 18).

But our small birds cannot just sit out a long snowstorm. They have to find something to eat every day. That's because they have a super-short "just in time" supply chain: they store only enough fat to tide them through a single night. At first sight, this is weird. Why don't they have enough fat to keep them going through several days of bad weather, especially, as a bit of blubber will keep them warm, too? We know that birds can put on massive amounts of fat if they need to. After all, our ruby-throated hummingbirds ate voraciously in the last week before migrating south last September, so that nearly half their body weight was fat.

If you are a junco, a chickadee, a tufted titmouse, or a cardinal, getting "fit for winter" doesn't involve putting on fat. Their clever trick is to put on muscle, especially flight muscle. The flight muscle of our backyard juncos is a third bigger today than it was last June. This is not all the better to fly with but all the better to shiver with. Our little birds shiver in the cold but, unlike you and me, they don't jiggle as they shiver. As the snow fell, the juncos were motionless in the dead redbud branches by the garage, but they were very busy working their central heating system: repeatedly twitching their flight muscles to create heat. Yes, our winter birds are with us because they are super-athletes.

Surviving the winter is all about getting calories to fuel the muscle central heating. Our feeding stations were well visited by all the usual customers in brief snowstorm lulls, every bird on its life-or-death mission to stock up for the coming night. But it is easy to imagine a bad luck day when this strategy could fail—and the first failed day would be the bird's last day. These birds are the ultimate survivors, and they have fallback solutions. One (used fairly regularly) is to lower their standards. Turn the central heating down a few degrees to reduce the calorie demand. When our chickadees turn down their central heating, they may be a bit sluggish, but they still have a good chance to escape a night predator or to move up and away from gradual buildup of falling snow. Last resort is torpor—to pretend, even briefly, to be a chipmunk, let the body temperature drop so low that the bird cannot be roused. Obviously this is dangerous in lots of ways, but both chickadees and juncos can do it. I know of only one bird that routinely hibernates like a chipmunk. This is a tiny nightjar called the common poorwill, which spends the winter under piles of rocks. You won't find the common poorwill in our backyard. It is a western US species that gets as far north as Canada in the summer and overwinters in the extreme Southwest of the US and in Mexico. The poorwill hibernates to reduce its demand for calories; it isn't cold.

It's about time to get to the second half of the title of today's letter. Yet again, it is about the relative of an African weaver finch that decided to try its luck as a companion of that descendant of an African ape. The Bumpus event happened to a flock of English (aka house) sparrows in the vines of the old library at Brown University in the state of Rhode Island. On February 1, 1898, there was a ferocious storm: perhaps, like the storm of February 1, 2021, it was a Miller B nor'easter. The 1898 house sparrows presumably tucked in their feet and heads and huddled together—the colder it got, the closer and larger the huddle. But the vine was not the best place to take shelter, and 136 birds were dislodged and knocked senseless to the ground. The rest is biological history.

The sparrows were picked by Hermon Carey Bumpus, professor of comparative anatomy and renowned for his obsession with shooting and stuffing animals. For his 136 sparrows, he diverged from this routine in two ways. First, he checked how many revived, and then killed 'em all and measured them. Professor Bumpus found that the sparrows that survived were smaller, weighed less, and had longer legs than the ones that died. Really unexpected, but all his numbers have been published. Over the subsequent century and more, birdy statisticians have pored over the Bumpus sparrow data. They have sliced and diced the data in different ways and reached lots of different conclusions. I think that tells us more about statistics than sparrows. To my mind, the truly successful sparrows were the ones in the most sheltered places in the vine that didn't get dislodged and end up being stuffed by Professor Bumpus.

I tell you all this because our English sparrow flock in the forsythia hedge at the bottom of the road has been conspicuous by its absence at our bird feeders this week. Much of the forsythia hedge is under snow, and it is a far smaller and less protected place to live than it was this time last week. We have checked it out every day since Wednesday. There are sparrows there, but the chatter is much diminished, and we have seen just a few birds. I fear that last week's snowstorm was a Bumpus event for the forsythia hedge sparrow population.

February 14, 2021

FINDING THEIR VOICE

Over the last week, we have witnessed a very welcome change in our backyard. We have hosted one, probably two Carolina wrens all winter, possibly the same pair that nested with us last summer. Time and again throughout the winter, including breakfast time this morning, we have witnessed the Carolina wren routine. Almost invariably, a single wren comes to the bird feeder, always from the privet hedge border with our western neighbor. It feeds adeptly on the suet block, regularly repositioning itself from top to side to bottom, and angling its incredibly flexible neck as it pecks. It also enjoys any breadcrumbs that we put out onto the snow-covered deck. It scoops each morsel into the side of its curved beak as it hops along.

But this week was different. As well as visiting us for nosh, the Carolina wren has broken into song on several days. Truly a buzz of exhilarating virtuosity—and then, as described perfectly in David Sibley's *Field Guide to Birds of Eastern North America* (Sibley 2003), a three-note rolling chant (pidaro—pidaro—pidaro—pidaro, on and on). In the cold, clear air, the wren's song reverberates around the yard, telling the world and every other wren from Carolina that this piece of real estate is "mine, all mine." A little farther up the road, the next Carolina is doing the same. Walk a little farther and there is another Carolina. Before I move on to other things, I should add that the Carolina wren does not come only from the Carolinas. We are right at the northern end of its range, which extends through the eastern part of the country down to Florida, eastern Texas, and even northeastern Mexico.

So what are the other things that I want to move on to? The Carolina wren is not alone. In the sunshine we have enjoyed during this last week, several other birds have found new voice. The call of our male cardinal has, all of a sudden, become more complex. Whether in our forsythia bush or on the fence, he accompanies his regular wintertime pip-pip with whistles and then chewee-chewee, and his plumage is now oozing with testosterone-fueled scarlet brilliance. The Mrs. (and it appears to be the same pair as nested with us last summer) has, similarly, smartened up with luscious red trimming to her tail and an almost fluorescent red beak.

All of this is so appropriate for this Valentine's Day letter. Interestingly, though, it is not new love but the winter-long pairings that are getting into shape for the breeding season. Other monogamous species have also been in evidence. That mostly means woodpeckers. Our smallest woodpecker, the downy (about the size of a yellowhammer or wagtail), has started some tentative drumming. Our largest woodpecker, the pileated (black and as big as a crow), has been flying in circuits either singly or as a pair, calling cuk, cuk, cuk... The tufted titmice pairs also stick together through the winter, and the first pee-ter's have rolled out across our backyard during the last week.

What has inspired this preparation for summer? I can assure you it is not the weather. Our world is white. Since the Miller B nor'easter at the start of the month, the temperatures have stayed firmly below freezing, day and night. The occasional glorious sunshine that we have enjoyed in the last week has been cold, routinely teens Fahrenheit and subtract five to ten degrees for wind chill. The clear skies have meant plummeting nighttime temperatures. We have also had snow every now and again, sometimes forecast accurately and sometimes not, and often several inches at a time. There have been times when we have looked from our sunny yard across to diagonal lines of heavy snowfall obscuring the line of southwest hills—and other times when snowfall has concealed the outline of our southwestern neighbor's house. With no snowmelt at all, this fresh snow is simply add-on, blurring or obliterating the path of human footprints from the kitchen to the composter by the privet hedge.

We can all agree that our Carolina wrens, cardinals, woodpeckers, and tufted titmice are not responding to spring weather. Nor are they fueled by any new source of food or sign of spring on the ground. Don't think about early spring flowers, not even snowdrops. The bulbs are safely blanketed under more than a foot of snow. The only possible inspiration is day length, now increasing by about three minutes a day. Dawn today was at 7 a.m., and sunset is closer to 6 p.m. than 5 p.m. Somehow these birds have what it takes to invest in the coming breeding season while still in the grip of grueling winter temperatures with ever-declining food supply.

Another big event of the week has been the American robins. We haven't seen any robins in the backyard for months. Late last fall as the supply of insects and worms declined, the robins abandoned us, either migrating south or retreating into local woodland for richer pickings of winter food, mostly berries. Our robin event happened on Thursday morning, in the middle of an unpredicted snowstorm. Suddenly there was a lot of noise and activity in our neighbor's locust tree and our crab apple tree. Through the falling snow, I could see about two dozen robins, mostly males, flitting about and calling to one another. Our male cardinal was attracted to the commotion and pipped gently from the pin cherry, just in front of my work desk. Then the blue jays came in noisily, as always needing to be in the know about anything that happens. Although the robins didn't appear to be fussed by any of this attention, they flew off in concert about ten minutes later. Then the cardinal and blue jays returned to their snow shelters . . . and I got back to work. Since then, we have seen a robin flock (the same one? who knows) career through our backyard on several occasions.

We are confident that these robins are not migrating north to set up for the summer. These are the small flocks that decided to stay north in the winter. The reason for our confidence is that robins don't pair up till spring, and it is mostly males who stay north in the winter. Our visitors are mostly males (black, not gray, heads and a much brighter orange breast than females). We think that they are on the move because they are hungry. Their woodland food of juniper, hawthorn, and holly berries is declining and they are checking out fresh habitat for anything not yet eaten. Fruits that were too distasteful to bother with last fall are now in high demand. Our yard has very little to offer, just a few privet, *Berberis*, and pin cherry berries, all wizened and well past their sell-by date, but other properties have good crops of the bitter viburnum berry, and outside a nearby house, there are several small trees with a long-neglected crop of small black fruit. We are frustrated in our attempt to identify this tree, but the newly arrived robin flocks have congregated around these trees and they are feasting with gusto.

February 21, 2021

THE DAILY CROW COMMUTE

Before I tell you about our flocks of crows, I need to set the scene. At this time of year, our backyard world is like a black-and-white movie from the 1950s. The ground is white, the snow-plowed roads are black or gray, the skies are mostly gray, and the bare branches of the black walnut and maple trees appear black or gray, depending on the light. Even the green needles of the snow-covered branches of the Norway spruce that towers over the garage and the small hemlock at the bottom of the yard look gray in our black-and-white world. The American crow is a perfect fit. It is about eighteen inches long and black from tip to toe—not just all its feathers, but its beak and its legs, all black. No wonder flocking crows played such a large part in Alfred Hitchcock's black-and-white horror movie *The Birds*.

During most of the year, we see the occasional crow in our neighborhood. I have always thought that our Norway spruce would be an excellent spot for a crow's nest, but there have been no takers so far. At the turn of the year into January, crows become more obvious, and they are center stage during February. Then they return to nothing more than cameo appearances in our backyard life by mid-March. During the day in February, the crows come and go. Some days they are cawing loudly in the large trees bounding our backyard or on the electricity wires at the front, usually in a group of two or three, but occasionally down to a singleton or up to a party of six birds. Other days it appears they don't visit us at all during the day. None of this is so very special.

The special bit is at the start and end of the day. Soon after dawn, as we look south from the breakfast table, we see a steady procession of crows flying from due west to due east. They fly comparatively low, at about the line of treetops, and their flight is steady and purposeful. They know what they are doing. Some days we see just a few individuals, other days it is an endless stream of these big, black birds silhouetted against the dawn light. I think it just depends on whether we happen to be watching at the start, middle, or end of the crow morning rush hour. Then in the dusk of the evening, there is the return commute, from east to west.

Who are these birds, and what are they doing? Luckily, I don't have to do much detective work, because the American crows in Ithaca have been studied for many years, in particular by a great colleague, Anne Clark at Binghamton University. Some years ago, Anne and I ran a conference together, and when we weren't fussing about speakers, advertising, and so on, we chatted about her fascinating work on the social life of "her" crows, each individually labeled with leg rings and wing tags.

Even so, a little detective work is helpful. Clue Number One is that many of the crows that visit our neighborhood in the summer and fall are ringed and tagged. They are residents and they have busy social lives centered on the family and a well-defined home base. The group comprises the parents, who build a new nest of sticks each year, plus offspring that hang around for several years before setting up independently. Clue Number Two is that rather few of the birds we see during the day in winter are ringed and tagged—and, if we were to check carefully, I am sure that this would also apply to the birds on the daily commute at dawn and dusk. This is because we have a massive influx of winter visitors, escaping the greater rigors of the Canadian winter. Anne and her colleagues tag only the year-round residents. The winter visitors are like the human "snowbirds" who spend the summer in New York and New England and the winter in Florida, except that the snowbirds of the crow world spend their summers 10 to 20° latitude farther north than the snowbirds of the human world.

So, what are the flocks of crows-from-Canada doing? They spend their nights in roosts of thousands of birds at a few locations, mostly in town, and then go off to spend the day feeding elsewhere. One of the main roosts, with an estimated ten thousand birds, is a bunch of trees just behind the Ithaca ReUse Center on Elmira Road at the southern end of town. By day, there are good pickings in the agricultural fields and the Reynolds Game Farm, where pheasant are raised, just to the southeast of the city boundary. Presumably, the crows we see during the middle of the day at this time of year are the individuals or small family groups that stop off to check out the menu in the suburbs. The evening crow commute back to the Ithaca ReUse Center is preceded by a get-together in the late afternoon. Last Tuesday afternoon, we watched one of these get-togethers in the trees up the road. There were hundreds of crows, all jostling around and making a great racket. After an hour or so of this, they fly off in concert to the roost.

What do the local crows think of all this? Most of the time, most of the tagged and ringed residents just stay at home, ignoring the antics of the crows-from-Canada. Occasionally, some individuals will join the pre-roost fun and, very occasionally, they will go the whole hog and indulge in a sleepover at the communal roost.

Why is it all so complicated? Perhaps our residents have places in their territories where they are well protected from the great horned owls and raccoons, but the winter visitors have no assured home for the night. So they group together in large numbers—and Elmira Road has the added advantage of streetlights so they can see any predators in good time. The motivation for our winter flocks of crows bears no resemblance to Alfred Hitchcock's *Birds* movie in California; and it is a far cry from the murderous intent of the carrion crows and rooks in the original Daphne du Maurier "Birds" story based in Cornwall, UK.

As well as our daily crow events, we have had a once-off big event this week. It concerns the red squirrel. On Monday morning we didn't see the red squirrel doing its daily round of dawn checks. Instead, it had company. Yes, two red squirrels chasing around the trees with amorous intent. Business done, the red squirrels returned to their determinedly antisocial lives. The female's offspring will be born in just over a month's time, she will raise her family alone, and her young will be off and away as soon as they are mature. What a different world from the close and enduring bonds of crow society.

February 28, 2021

PERIWINKLE FOR TEA

On Wednesday, temperatures rose to the dizzy heights of 50°F (10°C). In intermittent sunshine, the backyard was noisy with the continuous drip-drip of melting snow and the occasional thump as an icicle fell or a mass of snow slipped off the roof of our or a near neighbor's house. After Wednesday, we have had more time above freezing, and so we have much, much less snow. Our little box hedge has reappeared. We can see the top of the juniper bushes. Our crab apple tree, which divides into two main trunks about a foot above ground level, no longer looks like two trees planted close together.

The daily freeze-thaw cycle of the last few days has created perfect conditions to tap maple trees for syrup. There will be many people doing just that—both commercial outfits and hobbyists, including someone just up the road. For the rest of us, this time of year gives us hope that those sleeveless shirts and shorts at the back of the cupboard may not, after all, be clothing for a different universe. On Wednesday, we were able to go out without hat, gloves, and scarf. Even that felt strange, almost inappropriate. The birds are telling us that change is afoot. The cardinals are calling incessantly, the mourning doves have started to coo to each other, and the blue jays are telling the world all about it. Yesterday I had my first 2021 sighting of a turkey vulture wheeling high in the sky above the backyard. I am sure we will have many more views of these amazing birds in the coming days, as they return from winter quarters downstate and farther south.

But winter is far from done. It is still a tough world, and finding enough food to keep warm is top priority. This applies particularly to the white-tailed deer. Throughout most of the year, our local deer forage between dusk and dawn, but recently they have been out and about throughout the day. Indeed, as I write on this Sunday midmorning, I am watching a group of deer taking bites from the tips of the twigs of maple and redbud saplings as they make their desultory way along the edge of the snow-covered lawn of our northern neighbor.

In the last week, we have also seen the deer foraging with great gusto on the steep south-facing bank at the front of a house down the road. The snow on this bank has melted fast in the bright sunshine. The deer paw at the snow to expose the vegetation beneath and then munch and chew vigorously. Unmistakably, they are feeding on our neighbor's periwinkle, which is more widely known as vinca here. Periwinkle is planted very extensively as ground cover because . . . it is toxic to deer. You can find plenty of websites assuring you that deer will not eat vinca. This is true and the reason why our neighbor has the wonderful periwinkle bank, with many purple flowers in the spring. But at this time of year, the deer must have decided that it is better to suffer the side effects of the vinca alkaloids (reportedly including stomach cramps, low blood pressure, and nausea) than to go hungry.

Despite their dietary difficulties, our local group of deer are looking much healthier today than in late February of some previous years. They are inescapably elegant animals, with their black-fringed ears, and white margins to their black muzzle and eyes. When flustered, the deer snorts and chases away, raising its tail like a flag to reveal its bright white rump and underside of its tail. It is very likely that our local group of six individuals comprises two does and their offspring of last summer and possibly the previous summer. At least the numbers fit the information in our "mammals bible," *Mammals of the Eastern United States* (Whittaker and Hamilton 1998), which tells me that white-tailed deer have either singletons or twins once a year, and juveniles stay with Mom for up to two years, but no longer. The males live separately in so-called buck groups, except during the rutting season in the fall, and these groups are presumably just as hungry as our local family group.

All of this is happening outside of our backyard. We consider this a major success story—so far. Our backyard has all sorts of winter goodies for the deer. We know from previous years that the deer would particularly enjoy the buds of our viburnum bush and the lower branches of our redbud. We also know that spraying these plants with our bad egg–smelling deer spray has no effect at all at this time of year. Perhaps the bad smell and taste are less obvious in the cold, and perhaps the deer are so hungry that they don't care if their food stinks of bad eggs. The greatest winter deer threat is for the three hemlocks that we planted at the back of the yard. I don't mean the European hemlock of the carrot family and the cup of hemlock tea that Socrates famously drank, but the eastern hemlock of North America, a magnificent conifer in our local forests. Hemlock is another of those plants that deer totally ignore for most of the year, but I suspect that they would prefer hemlock to periwinkle today. We have four high poles positioned around the hemlock trees and a large green net in the garage. We are at the ready to cover our hemlock in netting at the first sign of deer in the backyard.

There are two reasons for our so-far-success story: fences and snow. The suburban deer flourish because there are no fences. They can wander at will through an endless parkland because, by and large, no physical barrier marks where one backyard ends and the next begins. The occasional homeowner puts up a ten-foot-high fence against deer, but this is rarely at the edge of their property, but rather designed to protect an inner sanctum of vegetables, tulips, or hostas. For better or worse, we have played it the British way. We have put up a five-foot fence around the edge of our backyard, to give us a little privacy as we drink our afternoon tea etc. and to provide a not-insuperable obstacle to the deer. A deer can jump our fence if needs must, but why bother? We regularly see deer ambling along the outer side of our fence—and treat that as a victory in our lives! We are convinced that the best way to reduce deer in our neighborhood does not involve guns, contraceptive baits, or coyotes. It is to start the fashion of British-style gardens with garden fences.

But we are possibly entering the time of greatest deer risk for our backyard. The deep snow has provided protection against access along the drive from the front. Now the snow is melting, and a determined group of deer could pick their way to the viburnum and hemlock. They have small brains and set ways, and we are just hoping that the periwinkles and twigs of our (de)fense-less neighbors' yards will keep the deer going till the spring.

March 7, 2021

SNOW FLEAS

March came in like a lion, with swirling snow and nor'westerly winds gusting to fifty miles per hour on Monday the first. Tuesday was bitterly cold in brilliant sunshine and a perfectly blue sky. We had a brief reprieve of above-freezing temperatures on Wednesday before returning to the freezer for the rest of the week. The regular bouts of snowfall have all been forecast as "less than an inch expected." That has meant anything from a light dusting, needing nothing more than a quick flick of the car windscreen with a brush, to half an hour of snow shoveling and ice scraping. We are glad and grateful for the repeated visits by a city snowplow, which trundles noisily up and down the street.

You could say that Ithacan snow comes in three styles. There's the light powdery stuff that, when you kick it, whooshes into the air with millions of tiny flakes sparkling in the sunshine. Then there's the heavy, soggy stuff that, within seconds, soaks any foot that isn't protected by a fully waterproofed boot. A minority of students wander around in trainers, and it must be like walking barefoot in cold puddles. And finally, there is the snow we have today. Kick at it and you will stub your toe. Our world is dominated by a weeks-old bedrock of hard, iced-over snow. New snow just freezes solid, adding to the bedrock. Actually, these three types of snow are a simplification. I won't elaborate beyond saying that the claim of fifty different types of snow in the Inuit vocabulary seems totally plausible to me.

The prime backyard event of the week relates directly to snow. It was Friday midafternoon when I went out to check for any sign of the snowdrops or winter aconites that grow between the maple tree and the privet hedge. I stepped carefully in our path of icy footprints to the composter, only to find—of course—that the Place of the Snowdrops and Winter Aconites is under several inches of crusty snow. I thought immediately of the skunk cabbage, which grows abundantly in wet places in the woods around here. This plant is very special because it flowers in March, possible only because the emerging flower shoot gets so hot that it melts the snow as it pushes its way up. For the sake of accuracy, the skunk cabbage is not a cabbage, it is an arum—like Lords and Ladies. And it makes heat by the same process as in mammalian brown fat. (Brown fat is how human babies keep warm and how our chipmunk warms up for its occasional wake-up during the winter.) But none of that is relevant to the snowdrops and winter aconites. which don't indulge in the skunk cabbage/brown fat trick. It is still too early for our first spring flowers. I looked up to the red maple tree, and then across to the hop hornbeam. The deep-red flower buds distributed all along the maple branches are still shut tight, and the little hornbeam catkins are no different from December.

And then I looked down. There was a patch of dirt on the snow close to the set of squirrel footprints that run from the end of the fence to the bottom of the bird feeder. The dirt was jumping up and down! It was unmistakable in the sunshine against the glinting snow. I went a little closer, using the squirrel trackway as best I could, to avoid any fresh disturbance to the snow cover. It was an enormous congregation of snow fleas. That needs some terminological unpacking, which I did later on Friday evening. First, I Google-checked for a standard term for a group of snow fleas, but there doesn't seem to be one. Somehow, "congregation" sounds better than a flock or herd of snow fleas. Second, a snow flea is no more a flea than a skunk cabbage is a cabbage. Snow fleas are springtails. A more productive Google check, specifically of the ever-helpful BugGuide.Net, told me that they were either *Hypogastrura harveyi* or *Hypogastrura nivicola*. My Failure of Friday was that I didn't work out which species it was—the antennae are shorter than the head in *Hn*, but longer in *Hh*, and *Hh* has anal spines. But that failure didn't interfere one jot with my pleasure in watching them literally springing up and down on their V-shaped tails. If you don't know your springtails, and you feel in the mood for a New Word of the Week, here it is. The tail of a springtail is a furcula, not to be confused with the furcula wishbone of a bird. Although snow fleas aren't fleas, they use the same resilin protein as in the hind legs of fleas to jump many times their own height, again and again . . . and again. As well as jumping up and down, the snow fleas feed on the microbes and bits of debris that fall onto the snow. These tiny jet-black animals are loaded with antifreeze, and I guess that they absorb heat from the bright sunshine to warm up enough for jumping around in the cold. We've checked the backyard for snow fleas over the last couple of days, and they seem to be gone.

As I watched the snow fleas on Friday afternoon, I was fully subscribed to the adage that you can't just survive an Ithacan winter, you have to embrace it (see January 24). But that frame of mind didn't last long. To be honest, we are all sick and tired of winter. Snow fleas aside, it is like living in Narnia under the thumb of the White Witch, where it is always winter and never Christmas.

All of which is a long way of saying that summer feels a very long way away, but it will win in the end. The cardinals know that.

At first light, our male cardinal is calling pip-pip-pip and chewee-chewee-chewee, alerting the world that this is his patch for the coming summer, and his ever-supportive Mrs. often joins in. In the world of cardinals, the winter days of peaceful coexistence (see November 29) are long gone. To give you a sense of his commitment to summer, singing duty starts at about 6 a.m., when it was just 18°F (minus 8°C) today, with similar temperatures through most of the last week. On Monday afternoon, our male cardinal was beating away an intruder in blizzard conditions of raging wind and snow. The intruder had a much more pronounced black mask around his beak, and I've not seen any male cardinal with those features since last Monday.

The cardinal is very special, because the confidence of most of our resident bird species that summer will come is much more weather dependent. At six o'clock on Wednesday morning, it was a bit warmer, meaning around freezing point, and the cardinal dawn chorus was accompanied by some faltering tufted titmice, chickadees, and mourning doves. Their spirits are willing for summer! We just need the wind to change direction from this persistent northwest.

As we ate breakfast this morning, I suddenly spotted a crow in the maple tree. It was reorganizing several nest-worthy twigs in its beak, and then it flew off to the west. Yet another sign that winter is on the run, even if it doesn't really know it yet. We just have to be patient.

March 14, 2021

ALL CHANGE

There was as much change in our backyard over the first four days of this week as in the last four months. For too long, one day could not be distinguished from the next except, possibly, by a slight change the height of the snow or shift in the color of the cloud. This week has been exhilarating!

It all started on Monday. The persistent northwest winds shifted through west to south. Temperatures rose from a nighttime 16°F (minus 9°C) to fridge temperature of 39°F (4°C). Not wanting to sound crazed, but that felt balmy. The snow started to melt in the bright sunshine. Walking gingerly along the thin margin of the lawn where the snow was gone, we could feel the still frozen ground below the just melted muddy goo. We were glad we made the effort because, there between the maple tree and the composter, were our snowdrops. Green shoots and swelling buds tinged in white. Hurrah! Our snowdrops have made it through the winter . . . as they do every year.

Monday was just the start. It has been sunny all week until today, most days of pure blue sky from horizon to horizon. Slowly but surely, the snow has gone. The grass is that dull yellow-gray of a winter survived, but it will soon be green again. By Tuesday I was even able to do my run on the drive. It was a bit silly because the remaining snow/ice in the shadow of the garage reduced my laps by a third, but it was lovely to be "back." I've not been able to do my daily run on the drive since mid-January, and my daily exercise in recent weeks has mostly been those inescapably grim 100 No-Equipment Workouts indoors (see December 13).

Tuesday was the perfect day to return to the driveway run. It wasn't just the sun on my face and the regular sounds of squawking blue jays, pipping cardinals, and teeth-chattering squirrels. It turned out to be a very special day. High in the sky overhead there were skeins of geese, all flying from south to north. Not just one or two skeins. They came in hordes, one after another. It was like those old newsreels of World War II fighter planes, wave after wave, with whirring engines against a backdrop of drumrolling victory music. The big difference, of course, was that the sky was a perfect blue and the sound was an endless stream of goose honks. The light was so good that the individual birds could be identified, many of the snow geese with their brilliant white wings, tipped in black, and the larger Canadas with brown wings and long black neck. Some of the skeins were Canada geese, others were snow geese, and some were mixed. The snow geese are on their long migration to their breeding grounds in the far North (see November 1). The Canadas could drop out at any point from here (where this species is also resident) to the southern reaches of Baffin Island. After the amazing hours-long display on Tuesday, it has been very quiet on the Goose Front, just the occasional single skein silhouetted against the sky or the faint sound of honking.

Things were starting to heat up. By midday Wednesday, it was 55°C (13°C), the winter aconites and crocuses were emerging in the soggy snowmelt, and some of the snowdrops were in flower. I could run the full drive, albeit with some fancy footwork between patches of remaining snow, and I didn't bother with hat or gloves.

The main entertainment for this run was not geese but an aerial engagement with the enemy. Three red-tailed hawks were moseying around. They must have been migrants, stopping off for a rest on their journey north. Although red-tails are resident here, we are pretty close to the northern limit of their year-round range, and red-tails are summer visitors through much of Canada. It was very clear that the local birds were perturbed, keen to make it clear that this is not a suitable neighborhood for a red-tail pit stop. The blue jays were making a racket, the little birds were not in evidence. In the end, a crow took matters into its own hands. As I trotted along the drive, it flew toward one of the red-tails, calling loudly. Initially, the red-tail turned a blind eye, but the crow was having none of it. There were the two birds, flying overhead so close that a single misstep with a wingbeat would have meant a collision. As the red-tail twisted and turned in the air, so did the crow in perfect split-second synchrony, screaming loudly. The end of the story was inevitable. The red-tails left us, the blue jays applauded in loud squawks, and before my run was done, we were back to the sound of titmouse Pee-ters and Carolina wren pidaros.

Thursday was the best day of the week, a miraculous 61°F (16°C). That sounds a bit over the top. The record temperature for that day is 70°F in 1977, but it felt miraculous! My run was in shirtsleeves, our aconites were in flower, and farther up the road, we saw the first honeybees of the season. There was another sign of spring at breakfast time. As if coming from nowhere, a woodchuck trotted along the side of the privet hedge, slipped under the fence, and was gone. This was right on cue because woodchucks emerge from their long winter hibernation at this time of year, even though there is precious little for them to eat. For a healthy woodchuck, that is okay because it should still have some remaining fat reserves laid down last summer to help out for a month or so. All the same,

I went out directly and sprayed the emerging violet leaves on the eastern wall with some bad egg spray (see May 24), just in case.

Of course, all of this couldn't last. The wind turned gustily to the north on Friday, and we have been downhill since then. In fact, it is snowing as I write. But the clocks went forward last night, and the day length is increasing rapidly with the equinox coming up soon. Inescapably, the cat is out of the bag and the genie out of the bottle. Summer is on its way.

But just as there is time's arrow, there is also time's cycle. This weekend we have started the annual conversation about whether it is time to take down the bird feeder. The marauding house sparrows are much fewer, usually two or three, presumably reduced by the Bumpus event last month (see February 7), but they are troublesome. We have come full circle, back to the same dilemma as exactly a year ago.

Postscript

I have always known that having access to nature on my doorstep is important to me. But I only started to ask the simple question "Why?" when I began to write my letters about the backyard. As the weekly writing progressed, I came to understand that engaging with the natural world involves much larger issues than just me and my backyard. I recognized explicitly that these interactions enrich our sense of well-being, give us the opportunity to enjoy natural history, and provide a route for us to promote wildlife. These three activities are mutually enhancing, creating what I call the "circle of natural connections" (see the first figure). This circle is just as relevant for time spent in a suburban yard or city park as in wild places.

How the Circle of Natural Connections Works

The ideas encapsulated in the circle of natural connection provide a framework for my year of letters about my backyard, and they offer a way to build the natural world into our day-to-day lives. Here I consider the three elements of the circle in turn, and then I address some practicalities.

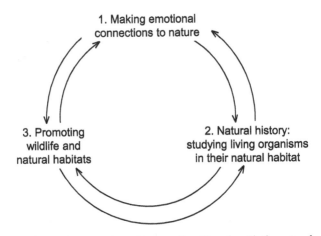

The circle of natural connections. Our emotional bonds with the natural world, the study of natural history, and our actions to promote the natural environment are connected and mutually reinforcing.

Making Emotional Connections to Nature

Humans have always had an emotional connection with the natural world (see step 1 in the first figure), but the relationship is neither consistent nor simple. On the one hand, we perceive nature as nurturing and life-giving: we are totally dependent on the habitable conditions that exist on this planet and on natural resources for everything that we eat and drink, and for all that we make. On the other hand, the natural world is a hazardous place that is inhabited by dangerous and venomous creatures and is the source of countless catastrophes, from storms and droughts to earthquakes and pestilence (see the top row of the second figure). For many of us, this tension is compounded by a profound anxiety that human activities are destroying natural habitats, driving other species to extinction, and disrupting the climate. Reliable science tells us that these anxieties are well founded. In parallel, our links

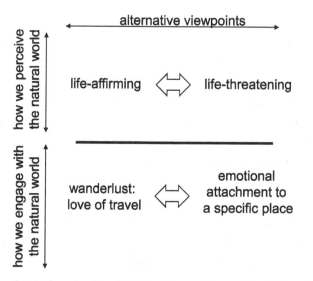

How we relate to the natural world. We hold contradictory views (*left and right*) about how we perceive the natural world (*top*) and engage with the natural world (*bottom*).

to the natural world are being eroded. The United Nations' report *World Urbanization Prospects* (2018) observes that more than half of the 8 billion humans alive today live in cities, and many people lack day-to-day contact with the natural world.

We are also contradictory in the ways in which we engage with the natural world (see the bottom row of the second figure). We are an adventurous species with a compulsive desire to explore the world. Our wanderlust must surely be part of the explanation for why modern humans dispersed—on foot—from their homeland in sub-Saharan Africa to colonize every habitable continent of the world over a period probably no greater than sixty thousand years. Our wanderlust also underlies the widespread misperception that engaging with the natural world has to involve traveling long distances to exotic habitats rich in wildlife against a backdrop of awe-inspiring scenery. The trillion-dollar tourism industry milks our wanderlust impulse.

Most people, however strong their wanderlust, also have an emotional connection to the place where they live or have lived previously (especially in their childhood). Environmental psychologists describe this bond as "place attachment" or "a sense of place." There is now good evidence that specific places promote our sense of identity and contribute to our physical and mental well-being. A very common focus of place attachment is a familiar green space, whether a yard, an urban park, or a more natural landscape, to which we have regular access. Spending time in these places is calming and restorative, promoting our perception that the natural world is life-affirming. We also have the strongest commitment to find out more about these special places, and the organisms that live there, and to care for and preserve them. This should be no surprise. Humans evolved in continuous contact with nature, not in a concrete cityscape.

Finding out about living organisms in their natural environment is the second step in the circle of natural connections (first figure). It is an activity of observation, using the senses of sight, hearing, and smell, and then interpreting those observations to identify living creatures and understand their habits. Some practitioners like to include landscape and weather in the study of natural history, drawing attention to the interconnections between living creatures and their physical environment.

Engaging in Natural History

Engaging in natural history enhances our appreciation of the natural world. Getting into nature is much more rewarding when we can recognize the creatures around us and know something about their habits. If this sounds daunting, don't worry! Natural history is a supremely "forgiving" activity that does not require a certain minimal level of expertise to be enjoyed. Each step taken leads to another step, to observe and find out about the natural world, and every step is fun. Even a casual interest and a little knowledge of the creatures living in our local patch can dramatically promote our emotional connection to the natural world, which in turn inspires a greater interest in natural history. This is how the circle of natural connections works (first figure).

It has never been easier to engage in natural history. We can make use of both excellent guidebooks that focus on different groups (birds, butterflies, trees, flowering plants, and so on) and Internet sites that provide photos, videos, and sound recordings. The accuracy of apps for identifying birdsong and plant species with a click of the cell phone is improving all the time. Similarly, we are spoiled for choice with books, magazines, and online articles that provide additional information about plants, animals, and fungi and their relationships. It is a straightforward matter to find answers to so many questions: Where are the snow geese going as they fly overhead, northward in March and back south in November? What is the basis for the name "snakeroot," a common wild plant that flowers in late summer? How are monarch butterflies affected by climate change?

Natural history writing is, however, far more than giving factual information. Many people interested in natural history also like to read—and, as I discovered for myself, to write. As I reported on the backyard events of the previous week every Sunday morning, I came to recognize that I was writing in the footsteps of the greats of natural history literature. Towering above all others was Gilbert White, one of the founding fathers of natural history as a discipline. Gilbert White was a "man of the church" (specifically, he was a Church of England curate) in the south of England during the second half of the eighteenth century, but he was as interested in the natural world as in saving souls. For example, his careful observations of the local birds revealed that some birds which could not be distinguished by eye have strikingly different songs, leading him to identify three small woodland species that we now know as the chiffchaff, willow warbler, and wood warbler. This achievement and many others are readily accessible to us because he discussed his ideas and findings in his extensive correspondence with two fellow enthusiasts, Thomas Pennant and Daines Barrington, over a period of twenty years. In 1789, this correspondence was published as a book, *The Natural History and Antiquities of Selborne* (White 1789). To this day, Gilbert White's natural history classic is fascinating to read, not only for its insights into the natural world but also because of its strong sense of place. Everything described by White took place in the village of Selborne (Hampshire, England), mostly in the beech hanger behind the small garden of the house where he lived. White's groundbreaking contributions to the discipline of natural history were anchored in his deep knowledge of, and connection to, his local patch.

Gilbert White's boundless enthusiasm for and curiosity about his small world of Selborne is inspiring. I felt a special link to his work in two further ways. The first is that my writing is in the form of letters. As for Gilbert White (White 1789), my letters are not a literary device; I really did write a letter once a week for fifty-two weeks. The other link is that, although the place attachment I describe in my letters is to my backyard in New York, Selborne is just fifty miles from where I grew up in the south of England.

Promoting Wildlife and Natural Habitats

Feeling an emotional attachment to a place and coming to know a little about the organisms that live there lead, inexorably, to a desire to look after the place and its inhabitants (see step 3 in the first figure). Our desire to be good stewards of the natural world is reinforced by the indisputable scientific evidence that human activities are causing habitat destruction, mass extinction, and climate disruption on a global scale. What can we do? There are many ways to contribute to taking care of the environment, and much can be achieved by the strategy to "think globally, act locally." We can't get much more local than the backyard! Professional scientists are increasingly recognizing that our yards can contribute to the protection of birds, insects, and other organisms. In particular, painstaking research of many conservation biologists is demonstrating how connected networks of yards can make all the difference for wildlife, especially for many once-common species that are now in decline.

Environmental stewardship is often projected as a complex and demanding activity, requiring sophisticated expertise and great dedication. This perception is accurate for the conservation of large areas, such as a river watershed or a mountain range, which include multiple habitats and are subject to myriad human uses and complex legal jurisdictions. But it is not complicated or time-consuming to foster wildlife in a backyard. In fact, being a good steward of a backyard is far simpler than being a competent gardener in the traditional sense. The key requirement is to adopt a mindset of engagement, to pay attention. Before you know it, you are firmly in place on the circle of natural connections. Any sense of effort or work disappears because you are enjoying the place, finding out about its natural history, and being a steward of a small patch of the natural world.

The Art of Strategic Neglect: Cultivating a Wildlife-Friendly Backyard

For many people, paying attention is a sufficient basis to engage with the natural world of the backyard or any other special place. But we are not all the same. Pragmatic people attach importance to the practicalities of how to promote wildlife in a backyard.

There are a few themes, but no rules, for managing a backyard to promote wildlife. The never-ending natural history treats of the backyard come primarily from the unplanned plant and animal life, what I call "the uninvited." This means that you don't need to be an expert, labor with the garden spade (and especially not with fertilizer and pesticides), or spend lots of money at the local garden center. By letting the wildlife come to you, you can enjoy the magic of wild creatures in your backyard without hard work. I describe this highly practical approach as strategic neglect.

Let me start with the neglect—I will come to the strategy a little later. I use the term "neglect" to mean that we should not strive to be neat and tidy. The attitude of letting things happen and take their course can run counter to much of traditional gardening practice, but it is most beneficial for wildlife.

Consider the tedious task of weeding. A weed is a plant that "shouldn't be there." Lower your standards, and weeds can become a feature of your backyard. For our backyard, the uninvited Virginia waterleaf provides a wonderful show of early summer white flowers (June 7); the nectar of the late-blooming calico aster flowers attracts myriads of insects (September 27); and even the admittedly ugly pileworts support elegantly sculptured mines of leaf-mining insects (August 23). We did not sow or plant the Virginia waterleaf, calico aster, and pilewort. They are all wild plants: uninvited guests that happen to flourish in our backyard.

Another opportunity for untidiness is not to cut back or remove herbaceous plants as soon as the flowers are over. The plants may not be aesthetically pleasing to us, but the fruits and seeds of garden plants and weeds are food for many creatures. Because animals are so varied in their food choice, a greater variety of seeding plants will support a greater diversity of animal life; and food spurned in the late summer and fall may be a lifesaver later in the winter when food is difficult to come by. In addition, senescing plants provide habitat for many insects and other invertebrates, which can be valuable food for predatory insects, spiders, birds, and mammals.

The lawn is the central feature of many backyards. Treating the lawn as a self-assembled plant community, not as a grass monoculture, promotes wildlife and makes our lives much easier. On our largely neglected lawn, bees and other pollinating insects work the summer flowers of clover and selfheal, while the cottontail rabbit adores the dandelion leaves. I don't pretend to be a great enthusiast for the plantain that invades some parts of our lawn, but plantain leaves are top items on the menu for many insects, including some flea beetles and weevils, and birds, especially the cardinals, feast on the plantain seeds. This may be anathema to the traditional gardener, but living with the plantains is a better option than digging them out (sounds like hard work) or applying a broad-leaf herbicide that would cause untold collateral damage to all the other non-grass plant species.

A neglected backyard may be less "in-your-face" colorful than a garden full of dahlias, hybrid roses, and bedding plants, with a lawn of perfect green velvet, but it is much more interesting and it is full of wildlife surprises.

Now it is time for the strategy of the neglect. The strategy is all about deciding how and when to intervene in the life of the backyard, and what to leave alone (or neglect). Some decisions are occasional and have large consequences. To plant some trees or bushes, and if so, what and where? To create (or fill in) a pond? Other decisions are quotidian, the decisions that shape day-to-day interactions with the local patch.

Here are a few examples of strategic intervention in our backyard. All summer long, we derive great pleasure from the marjoram that sprawls over the bank by the east fence. So we remove any competing plants from early spring to the onset of winter (April 5). We enjoy the sea of purple flowers of the meadow violets that flourish in the lawn, and so we delay mowing the grass till they have set seed in late May (May 3 and May 24); and the Deptford pinks that flourish on our lawn dictate the mowing regime in high summer (July 12).

There are no fixed rules about the strategy of what to neglect and how to intervene. It all depends on your priorities and prior experience of what works (or doesn't work) for your yard. Occasionally, decision-making is far from straightforward. In our household, much of the discussion about what to neglect and how to intervene has revolved around three issues: alien plants, the creatures that eat the garden plants, and feeding the birds.

Alien Plants in the Backyard

The backyard is a hotspot for aliens. Many garden plants have been introduced from other parts of the world, and non-native weeds flourish in the disturbed, often nutrient-rich yard habitat. In fact, the two categories overlap because some of the most pernicious invasive weeds were introduced in the nineteenth century as novelty garden plants (e.g., kudzu, Chinese privet, daylilies), and subsequently escaped into natural habitats. Other invasive weeds were cultivated for their supposed medicinal value (e.g., wild carrot and mullein), especially by the early settlers from western Europe, or were contaminants in agricultural products, such as crop seeds and animal fodder, brought in from other continents (e.g., spotted knapweed in a batch of alfalfa seeds imported from Siberia).

What is the most appropriate response to non-native plants? A laudable reaction is "native good, alien bad," meaning that any plant or animal that is non-native should be eliminated, wherever possible. There is, however, a growing recognition among professional ecologists that this perspective is unrealistic in two ways. First, some non-native plants are not all bad; they can promote wildlife as a food source (particularly nectar and seeds or fruits) or as a habitat where creatures can nest or overwinter. The second reason is that it is naïve to imagine that eliminating the aliens could restore pristine "natural" ecosystems. Humans have been managing wild places of this continent for at least nine thousand years, and the rapid and ongoing changes in climate, caused primarily by human activities, are creating new ecological states that support novel combinations of animal and plant species. Non-natives are increasingly part of the mix.

Returning to our backyard, we think carefully before planting non-native species, and we are indulgent about non-native weeds. But we are not consistent. For example, we planted some *Sedum spectabile*, a native of Asia, for its glorious late summer pink flowers loved by bumblebees (September 20). Similarly, we (and the wildlife) enjoy the uninvited wild carrot (August 2), originally from Europe, but we are vigilant in digging out the garlic mustard before it sets seed, so that it doesn't choke everything else out (June 7).

Some people will disagree vehemently about my message to be relaxed about alien plants in the backyard. I am relaxed about that. As I have said, different people have different priorities.

Managing the Plant Munchers

Just as we can learn to live with alien plants, we don't have to treat the creatures that eat the plants in our backyard as The Enemy. Plant-eating insects include the cicadas, crickets, and grasshoppers that serenade us in late summer (August 2 and August 16), and also caterpillars of butterfly species that we love to see flying around in the garden (August 23). They are also food for many of the garden birds and their nestlings, and for the fireflies (predatory beetles) that literally light up our midsummer nights (July 5).

With all these wonderful benefits conferred by plant-feeding creatures, perhaps we should not worry about holes in leaves and the occasional defoliated plant. Ecologists have discovered that most plants are tough and fibrous or well defended by toxins, and so are inedible for most animals. By and large, it is best to appreciate the plant munchers in the garden.

But some strategy is needed to deal with the hard cases. Some munchers can transform much-loved plants to stubble in minutes—that's deer and woodchucks for us. Certain insect species would wreak havoc if left uncontrolled—Japanese beetle is our annual foe. Fencing and netting can provide a degree of protection (February 28), but that is not always successful, and who wants their backyard to look like Fort Knox?

A difficult issue is whether and when to indulge in pesticides. Every garden center offers shelves of chemical warfare agents, all in colorful packaging and with claims of instant success. I believe that these products should be used only as a last resort, and then with great care. Why apply pesticides designed to kill plant-munching insects but that also kill many of the creatures that eat the plant munchers? Our backyard flourishes with just two regular interventions, neither of which involves traditional pesticides.

We use a spray containing decayed egg solids and garlic against deer and other mammalian munchers (April 12) and a highly specific sex pheromone to trap the voracious Japanese beetles in July (July 5). In some years, caterpillars of the spongy moth (also known as gypsy moth) are a serious defoliating pest, and we have controlled them very effectively with burlap traps, which are easy to construct and have no deleterious effect on any other insects (https://fyi.extension.wisc.edu/spongymothinwisconsin/pest-management-2/making-a-burlap-barrier-band-trap/). So far, our sole traditional pesticide purchase has been to eliminate carpenter ants that, on one occasion, decided to make their home in the wooden planks of our garage.

Feeding Garden Birds

Why feed the birds? There are two widely accepted reasons, both entirely valid. It is fun to watch the birds, and the food supplement can promote bird populations. As one delves, however, into the detail of feeding garden birds, it becomes complicated. What foods are appropriate, and when should they be provided? How can we manage feeding stations to minimize the spread of pathogens? Every bird lover's nightmare is that a nestling bird may choke to death on a peanut provided by its parent, or that their bird feeder is a hotspot for the spread of mycoplasma or other lethal disease agent. As Darryl Jones explains in his excellent book *The Birds at My Table* (Jones 2018), nestlings are rarely killed by peanuts, but disease transmission is a very real threat at feeding stations that are not kept clean.

As is evident from my first letter (March 22), we provide seeds and suet for the winter birds, but take down these feeders in early spring. In the summer, we have a garish red feeder that provides sugar solution for the ruby-throated hummingbirds. We have discovered that we are in a minority position. Many of our neighbors and friends supply seeds, suet, and other commercial products for the birds through the year. Our rationale is that our food is providing the calories that garden birds need to survive bitterly cold winter temperatures; and some scientific data support this position. As I discuss on February 7, the birds need to eat every day to stay warm during cold weather; and lack of food can be a major cause of winter mortality. At other times of year, a strategically neglected backyard should provide all the plant and insect food that the birds need. Even in the depths of winter, the bird feeder should represent just a portion (ideally a small portion) of the daily diet. An untidy, pesticide-free backyard offers the birds a balanced winter diet of seeds, overwintering insects, and so on.

We also need to consider the species that come to the bird feeders. We like to think that supplementary feeding "saves the birds." But this beneficial effect relates only to the birds that eat the food. Feeding the birds will tend to favor bird species that are bold, can access the food, and like the food. The species with populations inflated by the supplementary feeding may suppress other birds that do not make use of feeding stations. Our biggest concern is the house sparrows, which are über-competitors that oust other birds from the feeding stations, commandeer sheltered sites at night and in bad weather, and evict other bird species from nest sites in the summer. There is much scientific debate about the effects of supplementary feeding on house sparrow populations, but their negative effects on other bird species are not in doubt. My first letter (March 22) is dominated by the house sparrow problem, and our wintertime Sparrow Wars (December 27 and January 17) show that we care but that, frustratingly, we still lack a credible strategy. Perhaps a solution will become apparent next year.

Getting stuck into the practicalities of managing a backyard is one of the rewards of connecting with the natural world. Learning by experience how to promote wildlife enhances our sense of engagement with, and understanding of, the natural world. As the seasons come and go, there will always be new surprises, some familiar and some unexpected. That is the wonder of paying attention to your local patch.

Acknowledgments

I am immensely grateful to my relatives and friends who responded to my weekly letters with their natural history observations and photographs, brightening our lives through that first year of the pandemic. I particularly thank Andrew and Lesley Searle, Keaka and Nick Reid, John Colvin, Helene Marquis, Judy Raabe, and Lesley Smith. I also thank the American crow guru, Anne Clark, who kindly checked my letter of February 21 about crows, and Ann Hales for her thoughtful comments on the postscript. Two anonymous referees, Kitty Liu (editorial director for Comstock Publishing) and Jackie Teoh (acquisitions assistant at Cornell University Press) provided valuable recommendations that have made all the difference. I am also grateful to Karen Hwa and the production team at Cornell University Press who have translated my manuscript into this book. Most of all, I thank my husband, Jeremy Searle, the only person mentioned by name in my weekly letters. Jeremy protected my Sunday morning writing time against all comers for the full fifty-two weeks. He also gave me good advice throughout the project and displayed unfailing good humor when I ignored him. Most of all, Jeremy and I share an enthusiasm for all the animals and plants that inhabit and visit our backyard.

References

Comstock, Anna B. 1911. *Handbook of Nature Study*. Ithaca: Comstock Press. The original text was revised in 1939 and reissued in 1986 by Cornell University Press.

Del Tredici, Peter. 2010. *Wild Urban Plants of the Northeast*. Ithaca: Cornell University Press. Note that a second edition was published in 2020.

Elliott, Lang, and Wil Hershberger. 2007. *The Songs of Insects*. Boston: Houghton Mifflin Co.

Hardy, Thomas. 1878 [1985]. *The Return of the Native*. Reprint, London: Penguin Books.

Jones, Darryl. 2018. *The Birds at My Table*. Ithaca: Cornell University Press.

Mabey, Richard. 1996. *Flora Britannica*. London: Sinclair Stevenson.

McClintock, David, and Richard S. R. Fitter. 1956. *Collins Pocket Guide to Wild Flowers*. London: Collins.

Mitchell, Alan. 1974. *A Field Guide to the Trees of Britain and Northern Europe*. London: Collins.

Sibley, David A. 2003. *The Sibley Field Guide to Birds of Eastern North America*. New York: Alfred A. Kopf.

Sibley, David A. 2009. *The Sibley Guide to Trees*. New York: Alfred A. Kopf.

United Nations Department of Economic and Social Affairs: Population Dynamics. 2018. "World Urbanization Prospects 2018." Accessed November 21. https://population.un.org/wup/Publications/.

White, Gilbert. 1789. *The Natural History and Antiquities of Selborne*. There are many edited versions of this classic text. I can recommend Anne Secord, ed. 2016. Oxford: Oxford University Press.

Whittaker, John O., and William J. Hamilton. 1998. *Mammals of the Eastern United States*. 3rd ed. Ithaca: Cornell University Press.